4/26/2013

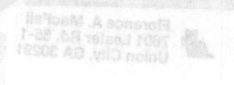

God's Champion

THE LIFE OF JOB

Robert W. Butler

WestBow
PRESS
A DIVISION OF THOMAS NELSON

WestBow Press books may be ordered through booksellers or by contacting:

WestBow Press
A Division of Thomas Nelson
1663 Liberty Drive
Bloomington, IN 47403
www.westbowpress.com
1-(866) 928-1240

ISBN: 978-1-4497-7766-1 (e)
ISBN: 978-1-4497-7767-8 (sc)
ISBN: 978-1-4497-7768-5 (hc)

Library of Congress Control Number: 2012922668

Printed in the United States of America

WestBow Press rev. date: 11/29/2012

Contents

What is the nature of spiritual reality?

Man falls short of God's perfection.

Good and evil are personal.

God is in control.

How can Job worship in the midst of tragedy?

He has a relationship with God.

He understands he is a steward.

He accepts that God is in control.

He walks by faith.

What is the nature of our spiritual battle?

Persistent and potentially progressive.

An attack on God.

Exists under God's control.

Uses human agency.

How can we comfort the suffering?

Our presence.

Our actions.

Our silence.

Preface

MOTIVATION

It would be fair to say I have been a reluctant participant in the process that generated this book. Several years ago, as I was coming to the end of preaching through Colossians, I was praying about which book to share with the congregation next. I felt a leading to preach through Job; I am prone, however, to be a little resistant to God's leading, and I found this was no exception. Mine was an older congregation; its members were dealing with enough of their own and didn't need Job's problems piled on, so I argued with God that they didn't need any more exposure to pain and suffering.

As God and I had this debate, God started to make very clear to me that this book was about Him, not Job. I knew the story of Job, but the thought that it was about God had never crossed my mind. Job had lost everything. His wife had criticized him. His friends had condemned him. God showed up and left everyone scratching his or her head. I began to read the book again a little skeptically, but I began to see how God is indeed the center of everything. He set the story in motion; He was the main topic of discussion in all the speeches; He clarified His perspectives about who was right or wrong. I stopped arguing with God and agreed to preach through Job.

After a few Sundays of teaching Job, I started to have people tell me I should turn my sermons into a book. Such comments had never happened before, and I dismissed them. Almost every other week, however, a different congregant would make the same suggestion. I began to wonder if it wasn't a conspiracy. Eventually, one of the members who had been a pastor told me my sermons on Job should become a book. God had my attention at that point. It was a conspiracy; God had used others to get my attention.

A year or so later, I transcribed a few of the sermons into chapters and followed a large publishing company's submission process. I am sure I received the most common response: the publisher encouraged me to consider another company. So the project resided unattended in my computer for a few years.

A couple of years ago, God seemed to be subtly asking, "Do you remember that project on Job?" I did, so I transcribed and edited more of my sermons. It was hard work. I asked my wife if she thought it was a good idea. Since it was going to cost time and money, I was reasonably sure I would get a negative answer. However, the conspiracy was still in full swing. Not only was she supportive, she encouraged me to do it.

When I was preaching through the book and getting feedback from members of the congregation, I think the single most significant idea they addressed was the nature of our relationship with God. Is it based on what God has done or what we do? Do I benefit from what God has done or what I do? While the questions were simple, the book of Job explores the depth and significance of the question. God said Job was right and his friends were wrong; I will remind the reader of this truth in many chapters of this book. If we lose sight of God's conclusion, that this book is about Him, we will not learn God's lessons. This is a book for those who want to know God better, especially those who want off the treadmill of religious performance.

RESOURCES

As I prepared my sermons each week, I referred to several commentaries. Some were books I had bought in the past; others were in digital format, and I refer to them on occasion. One is Matthew Henry's commentary entitled *An Exposition, with*

Practical Observations upon the Poetical Books of the Old Testament, published in Philadelphia in 1830. Another is Jamieson, Fausset, and Brown's *A Commentary Critical, Experimental, and Practical on the Old and New Testaments,* published in Grand Rapids in 1967. The digital commentaries I used are Adam Clarke's commentary, Barnes' Notes, and Keil and Delitzsch's *Commentary on the Old Testament.*

I did not quote any of these while I was preaching. When I use someone else's work when preaching, it is for illustration, not instruction. I did not cite any commentaries in writing this book. However, I thought it might be of interest to some to know what materials I used in preparation. Some of my conclusions are different from the commentaries.

I use the *New American Standard Bible,* updated edition, when I preach. All Scripture quotations, unless otherwise indicated, are taken from the New American Standard Bible, © Copyright 1960, 1962, 1963, 1968, 1971, 1972, 1973, 1975, 1977, 1995 by The Lockman Foundation. Used by permission.

Acknowledgments

This book never would have been written without many others who assisted along the way. I want to recognize four in particular.

The first is the late John Robbins, a bright light in my congregation who was in love with Jesus. He more than any other individual encouraged me to pursue this project. He made the recordings of the sermons and gave me a copy. Almost every Sunday he would tell me I should put the truths of God's grace and character I was presenting from the pulpit into a book. Sadly, he did not live to see the results of his encouragement.

The second is my wife, Bonnie Butler. At times I would question the sanity of continuing to write the book, but she would always encourage me to see the project to its end. When it came to the financial issues, she always said God would provide. Without her support, this book probably would not have been completed.

The third is my sister, Linda Malito. She has taught school most of her adult life and has been involved in a variety of churches and ministries. She read my draft for spelling, grammar, and the support of ideas. I have deleted and inserted material because of her questions and challenges; her insight was indispensable.

The fourth is a member of my congregation, Patty Vargas, who teaches our morning women's Bible study. She has written many skits for various congregational events and has demonstrated her writing skills and abilities with words in many ways. I asked her to read the draft for impact and tone, and her suggestions are also in the finished product.

Each of these individuals brought something significant to the completion of this book, and I am grateful for their contributions. I trust God will continue to use and bless them.

Introduction

Job: God's Champion

As we begin the study of Job, we should realize important facts about the book that will help us understand what God wants us to learn, as is the case with any book of the Bible—who the writer was, when was it written, and how was its structured. We will also make some comments about the other characters in the book as well as provide an idea about the purpose of the book. These will help answer the question about why Job is included in Scripture.

Let us start with some thoughts about when the events in this book would have happened. Job lived during an interesting time in history. He was a relative contemporary of Abraham, close in time but probably before Abraham lived. This would have been around the same time as Hammurabi and his famous legal code, the time civilization was developing in the Fertile Crescent and the Nile River region of Egypt. That would place the story around 2000 BC. One of the major factors in drawing that conclusion was the way wealth was enumerated then, in livestock. The nomadic nature of how the people in the book of Job lived also places this in the same cultural period of Abraham.

While written language existed at the time, oral tradition was a more common form of passing information from one generation to the next, so you may wonder who wrote it. The most common opinion is that Moses recorded these events as handed down through oral tradition. While it is possible these events could have been given by divine revelation, such a conclusion is not necessary for Job to be included in the

Bible. The vocabulary and grammar of the book indicate that the story's events preceded the life of Moses and depict a time more consistent with Abraham.

The next question would be how Moses heard the story. This is important, since the story, as best we can tell, comes from the western Fertile Crescent region, but Moses was born in Egypt and raised in Pharaoh's house by his daughter. As you may recall, he believed he was going to deliver the people of Israel from Egypt. At some point, he killed an Egyptian overseer and fled to the Sinai Peninsula in fear of his life. In the desert, he became a shepherd and married the daughter of a priest. Having lived in two different areas, Moses may have heard this story in Egypt, or he may have learned it during his time in the desert; there is just no definitive answer. It seems more likely the story would have been passed among priests and thus causes us to lean toward his learning the story from his father-in-law in the Sinai Peninsula.

That takes us to the question of who Job is. One line of thought believes he was a priest; as such, his experiences would have generated more interest and a possible explanation for the story's dissemination. Nevertheless, at the beginning of the story, we know very little about him. He was wealthy in livestock, and we quickly learn of a wife and ten children and many servants who oversaw his herds and lands. The longer life expectancies of that era would also be required for the totality of the events to unfold. So his time would have been closer to the flood and the subsequent rebuilding of civilization. There would have been a broader cultural understanding of God's expectations.

Before we begin our study, a little structure will also be helpful. The book of Job is divided into three parts. There is a short section at the beginning, another short section at the end, and a long section in the middle. In the first two chapters is some give-and-take between God and Satan that sets up the events that follow. The middle section, chapters 3 through 37, has several exchanges between Job and his friends, primarily Eliphaz, Bildad, and Zophar. It is generally believed that each was an influential man who came from a different area of the western Fertile Crescent area. The middle section includes three sets of speeches by Job's friends and his response. They condemned him and explained why he needed to repent and correct his behavior. To each of these, Job replied they did not understand who God was. Finally, Elihu challenged Job because the other three had failed to demonstrate his guilt. In the conclusion of the book, chapters 38 through 42, God spoke and clarified who was right and who was wrong. When we address the exchanges between Job and his friends, we will look at both speeches in the same chapter, which will allow us to reflect on the accusation and the response at the same time.

That brings me to the issue of why this story was included in Scripture. Job was not a Jew or a Christian, so there must have been something significant about this book to be included in the Bible. I believe the answer is fairly simple: God is revealing who He is. We must not place Job front and center in the story or the conflict with his friends because those things will lead us from the heart of God. All of Job's experiences are only the backdrop or context for the real story. This book is about God and His interaction in our world. It puts God on display: His character, nature, perspectives, and concerns. I believe this is the reason the book of Job has been preserved and included as a part of Scripture. We do not need more examples of suffering. We do not need confirmation that Satan, our friends, or other acquaintances will attack us. We need more of God. We need a greater understanding of the drama we call life and God's role in it.

These are significant-enough issues to have this story preserved in oral tradition and passed on for hundreds of years. These are significant enough to have Moses pen the story and preserve it in print. These are significant enough for the story to be included in the Bible. The God of heaven has declared who He is and that we can know Him. Before the cross and before Abraham, Job anticipated the resurrection. Before the cross and before Abraham, Job knew a personal relational God. Before the cross and before Abraham, Job knew his relationship was built on God's grace and not his own merit. The book of Job sets in motion all the great truths of the Bible because it is a book about God.

The last issue is that of assumptions. People color what they see, hear, or read with the assumptions they bring to those experiences, and the book of Job will be no exception. While there may be many worth discussing, I want to address only one. Are we going to assume God is obligated to protect or involve Himself in our fallen world? I believe the answer of Scripture is no. The Bible is a story about God choosing to invest Himself without obligation in the type of relationship He desires to have with us. God was not obligated to protect Adam and Eve from the schemes of the Serpent in the garden (Gen. 3:1). God was not obligated to protect Abel from Cain (Gen. 4:8). God was not obligated to provide for all humanity in the flood (Gen. 7:4). God was not obligated to keep Joseph from his brothers, his master's wife (Gen. 39:19–20), or fellow prisoners. God was not obligated to protect Egypt or Israel from the Death Angel (Ex. 12:29). God was not obligated to protect Israel, the godly or ungodly, from the consequences of David's choice (2 Sam. 24:12). God was not obligated to protect Shadrach, Meshach, and Abed-nego from the fiery furnace (Dan. 3:18). God was not obligated to protect Stephen from the crowd (Acts 7:59). Jesus told us His people would be persecuted until He came (Matt. 10:23); He did not promise protection. Jesus warned Peter about the temptation he would face from Satan, but he did not protect him from it (Luke 2:31). God is not obligated to protect us.

Throughout history, God's people have experienced the consequences of living in a fallen world. Natural disasters kill and destroy those who serve God as well as those who do not. Diseases kill indiscriminately, thieves steal, murderers take lives, and weather affects everyone. God is not obligated to protect jobs, children, health, or possessions. We will all experience the results of sin. God can and does intervene in the natural course of events, but He is not obligated to do so.

We do not control the actions of God; He operates for His own glory and does not share it (Is. 43:7). If God is obligated to act in response to our actions, decisions, or values, the glory is ours, not His. For grace to be grace, God cannot be obligated to act on our behalf under any circumstances. If we can obligate God to act on our behalf, we have something to boast about that is contrary to the teaching of Scripture (1 Cor. 1:29). He makes it clear it is His choice.

How do we apply this to Job? He lost his children to a natural disaster, his wealth to thieves and robbers, and his health to disease. Sin and Satan were and are responsible for all these misfortunes. Job's experiences were not unique. God was not and is not obligated to protect Job, you, or me from any of these. The question Job answers is, "Can my relationship with God survive the experiences of living in a fallen world?" If we think God is obligated to protect us from life, we will struggle because we have misunderstood Him and will certainly misrepresent the experiences of Job.

WOW!
AMEN

CHAPTER 1
The Challenge
Job 1:1–12

The book of Job can be a discouraging study. Our thoughts may quickly wander to loss, suffering, and condemnation. We may reflect on those we know who are struggling physically, emotionally, financially, or spiritually. The pains, hurts, and frustrations of life may consume our understanding of this book. Whether they are ours or a loved one's, they are strong influences. Job experienced all this and more. He lost all he had, even the support of his friends, who chided and reproved him. Yet the most significant frustration he faced was the contention he had failed God. Don't we feel that way sometimes? Job's life certainly contained an abundance of suffering and the challenge of friends; nevertheless, that is not the focus of this book. We cannot allow negative experiences or judgmental tendencies to distort our understanding of what God wants us to learn from the experiences of Job. This book answers the heart's cry, "Who is God? Can I know Him?"

This story is about the promise-keeping God of Adam and Eve, the rainbow-maker of Noah, and the friend who walked with Enoch. We have this book because it contains a wonderfully detailed description and personal illustration of God's awesomeness. The most basic truth we will see in

Job's life is the distinction between true biblical godliness and man-made religion. If we understand what God is declaring about Himself, we will avoid the foolishness of ideas that have permeated mankind's thinking since the beginning of time. This amazing book shows a stark contrast between the voices of men such as Job, who understood God as a God of relationship, grace, and mercy, and those with differing views. Some see God only as a holy, righteous adjudicator and someone they need to cower before. On the contrary, this is a glimpse into heaven and the greatness of God. The book begins with the spiritual backdrop for the earthly events in the life of one individual. I trust you will read this with a thirsty heart and a desire to know God better.

I encourage you to read Job 1:1–12, which set the stage, introduce us to the main character, and take us to heaven, where we find the background for the events that unfold on earth. This conversation between God and Satan about Job was the reason for the tragedies he was to experience. Satan asserted two points. First, Job served God only because he was blessed and protected. Second, if these privileges were removed from Job, he would curse God. Because of Satan's challenge, God chose Job to be His champion, to represent His relationship with humanity. God therefore granted Satan the power to remove all that Job possessed, but he was prohibited from harming him physically.

As we begin our study of these first twelve verses, I believe the appropriate question to answer encompasses the nature of our spiritual reality. We live in a physical world, but we also live in a spiritual world, the same world Job occupied. We need God's foundation as well as our own life experiences to make sense of the story that follows. The content of these verses needs to shape our understanding of how the physical and spiritual worlds interact. There are three truths in these verses that establish the nature of this reality from a biblical perspective; these concepts separate biblical Christianity from most religious thought.

Based on verses 1 through 5, the first truth we need to understand is that human beings fall short of God's perfection and are separated from Him. We learn this from Job's concern and his regular sacrifices (Job 1:5). Every person, on his or her own merit, cannot stand righteously before God. Each is guilty even if unaware of the condition. This was the concern Job had for his children, and it is a common theme in religious practices around the world. Paul tells us that humanity is aware of God's judgment and chooses not to worship Him (Rom. 1:18–23). Job's goal was a right relationship with God; he knew his standing with God was not dependent upon what he had, what he did, or who he was. While this may seem obvious, it wasn't clear to Job's friends, and this concept sets Christianity apart from other religious practices. As we consider the speeches with his friends, we will learn what Job understood about the sacrifice he was making and the basis of his relationship with God.

Some conclude from verse 5 that Job was fearful and worrisome. Without the next few verses, that might be a reasonable conclusion. He certainly had human and parental concerns. However, we do have the next scene in heaven between God and Satan. If we accept that God is correct in His analysis of Job, we have to conclude that those who think Job was fearful and worrisome are wrong. It should be obvious that those who accuse Job of moral flaws, character failures, or other behavioral misdeeds are in disagreement with God. As a fearful or worrisome individual, Job would be like most of humanity, not an example for God to mention or for Satan to note. God would not stake His reputation as a God of relationship and grace on such a person. This is a dispute with Satan about who God is, not who Job is.

At the end of the book, after all has happened, God held the same opinion of Job (Job 42:7). At issue in this challenge were the character of God and the nature of our relationship with Him. Is it built on things done (as contended by Job's friends), on things given by God (as contended by Satan), or on God's grace and mercy (as steadfastly declared by Job)? This is the key to understanding the book of Job and the God of the

Bible. Job is God's champion who demonstrated His gracious, merciful relationship with humanity.

While Job was a part of the physical world, he sought a proper relationship with the God who created it. This is evident from the sacrifices he made. As a righteous man with regular religious practices, he recognized sinful actions and their resulting separation from God. Some religious thought is premised on a different view of reality. Job's view, the biblical view, is significantly different from the view of those who believe that everything is essentially one essence and that our goal is to become one with it. That would be like the "force" in *Star Wars* or the merging of life in *Avatar*. This teaches that our uniqueness, our individuality, is the problem, the evil, we need to overcome. While the nature of reality is a profound philosophical discussion, biblically it is a straightforward declaration. God created it out of nothing, He made something exist and operate in its own right (Gen. 1:1). The world we experience and live in is the result of God's creative decisions. We are a unique creation in His image, and He desires to have a relationship with us. A biblical worldview must begin with God as the source of its existence.

Further, we are separate and separated from Him. These verses imply, and the story later demonstrates, that every individual has a choice. Job had the option to maintain his relationship with God or to take his wife's advice and reject God (Job 2:9). Nevertheless, God chose Job to be His champion in this epic battle with Satan because He believed His relationship with Job could withstand the most devastating trials of life.

We also learn in these verses that Job was a wealthy man with a wife and children. His wealth did not get him special standing with God. In the same vein, the fact he and his family enjoyed wealth did not get him special condemnation by God. On the other hand, his wealth got him condemned and attacked by Satan. His friends later condemned his loss of wealth. In terms of his relationship with God, his wealth was neither an asset nor a liability.

The same could be said for his family. Some believe that one's right relationship with God or the spiritual dimension comes through family or wealth. Later events certainly shatter these notions. Job's relationship with God was not dependent on his family or wealth. These provided nothing of merit for the relationship of his wife or of his children with God. Relationship with God is personal.

In verses 6 through 11, we see a scene in heaven. The life of Job had gotten the attention of both God and Satan. That fact leads to the second truth found in this text. Biblically, both good and evil are personal. God exists, as does Satan. They were aware of Job and the facts of his life. We learn later that God had a relationship with Job and that Satan was willing to be involved with his own agenda. Verse 6 says, "Now there was a day when the sons of God came to present themselves before the Lord." The sons of God (most believe these were angels) came before God to give an account of the things they had been doing. While they were before God, a former angel also made an appearance. It was Satan, referenced elsewhere in Scripture as the Devil (Matt. 4:1, 5, 8, 11; Eph. 6:11), Lucifer (Is. 14:12 in the KJV), the Prince of the Power of the Air (Eph. 2:2), and the Serpent of Old (Rev. 20:2).

God as presented in these verses was a distinct being, personal and relational. God as a unique being and involved personally with humanity was foundational to biblical Christianity. Other religious views believe God is an impersonal force that often tends to have a good and a bad side that need to be balanced. That is not biblical. A related notion is that God is everything and everything is God. Some see everything with spiritual power that men must appease: trees, rivers, even ancestors. These spiritual forces must be satisfied to experience blessing or there will be negative consequences. On the other end of the spectrum, some believe there is no spiritual dimension. The physical world is all that exists. Uniquely, the Judeo-Christian view sees God as personal.

The God of the Bible, the God of Job, needs to be God all the time—same expectations, same relationship. There is no spiritual comfort or certainty if God has changing standards and expectations. The Bible shows God is not confused or wavering. We must know God is God, the same forever. The book of Job communicates and supports this truth. Job's confidence in his relationship with God was founded on this assumption. You cannot be certain in changeable circumstances. The God of eternity, Creator of heaven and earth, is the same yesterday, today, and forever (Heb. 1:12; 13:8). We cannot face eternity with the certainty John wanted (John 21:31) if there are constantly changing standards and expectations. We could never know if we were right or wrong, pleasing or unpleasing to God, and neither could Job. God's statements could not be trusted because trust is built on an expectation of certainty.

God does not change; this was Job's assumption throughout the book. It underlay the disagreement with his friends. He contended he knew God and they were misrepresenting Him. If God changed, Job's declarations would not have substance because God could have changed his mind, standards, or expectations. If God changed, neither Job, nor we, could ever know if we were acceptable in His sight or pleasing to Him. If the rules change during life, or worse, after life, maybe we will not make it to heaven regardless of what the Bible says. The creator God of eternity must be unchanging, "the same yesterday and today and forever" (Heb. 13:8). A biblical view requires that the basis of the relationship Job had with God about 4,000 years ago must be the basis of the relationship we can have today. The belief in a changing reality will lead to either intolerance or indifference because it is an errant view of God and the world He created. Job's friends demonstrated intolerance.

Almost everyone has dealt with changing expectations that caused concern and frustration. They did in relation to my college experience. When I started at the University of California at Irvine in 1969, there was a well-defined graduation requirement. I expected to graduate four years later, having completed the prescribed course of classes. However, as I started the next year, they changed the requirements to graduate. It was not a big deal. There were three years left, and the changes were not all that significant. Unbelievably, when I started my third year, they changed the requirements again, and this time they were significant, and I had some concerns in my senior year about graduating.

I have also worked at a place where we joked, "If you don't like the rules, it's okay; they'll be different next week." Uncertainty is an uncomfortable place whether in life or with God. We need clarity and certainty to move forward with confidence at school, home, work, and church. Uncertainty produces confusion and frustration, but we can stand in the certainty of our relationship with God.

To explore the personal nature of evil, we need to turn our attention to God's adversary. A big problem for some in our world is their rejection of evil. They do not believe in a personal devil, considering him a figment of the imagination. They put him in the same category as Santa Claus or the Easter Bunny. Because some believe good and evil are a part of the same cosmic force, they do not see a fundamental difference between them. Others believe evil is the result of ignorance or greed, so their answer always involves more education or money. Others want to believe everything is contextual and relative; for them it's about the ends, not the means. History has shown these solutions and approaches fail the test of civility. Brutality and authoritarianism are the common results. Biblical Christianity should expect failed solutions when evil is ignored as the real problem.

God's adversary is active and effective. There is real evil, a real Devil with a personal agenda. According to these verses, the real-world events that follow are a stage for his spiritual battle with God. He is doing today exactly what he did in the book of Job. He is wandering around earth, attacking God's character, agenda, and people. This was not lost on the apostle Peter. In his first letter he tells us, "Be of sober spirit, be on the alert. Your adversary, the devil, prowls around like a roaring lion, seeking someone to devour" (1 Pet. 5:8). He is still seeking those he can devour. He may be making deals with God

7

regarding those he can take down, in his opinion, or at least attempt to destroy.

A heavenly event gives us a glimpse into this adversary's behavior; Revelation 12:10 says, "Now the salvation, and the power, and the kingdom of our God and the authority of His Christ have come, for the accuser of our brethren has been thrown down, he who accuses them before our God day and night." The previous verse tells us the one thrown down was Satan. What was he doing then? He was standing before God, making accusations against those who believed in Jesus Christ as their Savior. This underscores the importance of having an advocate with the Father (1 John 2:1). Jesus stands and declares the finished work of the cross. He produces the evidence that the blood has been shed and the penalty for sin has been paid. We have been forgiven. Yes, there is an accuser, and certainly we have an enemy. More important, we have a victor. Non-Christians need a savior. There is one who faced all the challenges of life and death and won (Heb. 4:14, 15). He withstood the accuser and went to the cross. While we were sinners, Jesus died for us (Rom. 5:8). He paid for our sins, and He stands before the Father on our behalf.

So far, these verses teach that people are separated from God because they fall short of His perfection. Next, they show the personal nature of good and evil. Verse 12 gives us the third truth about our spiritual reality. God, the one in charge, controls the spiritual as well as the physical. God is the one giving directions, the one to whom everyone is giving an account, the one who gave Satan permission. Without His permission, Satan had no ability to impact Job's life. God's actions demonstrate His control.

Let us apply that thought to the challenge at hand between God and Satan. God declared that Job was righteous and that there was no one like him on earth, while Satan contended Job's righteousness was due only to his possessions and God's protection. God knew that was not true. Whether Job was wealthy beyond our wildest imagination (as we meet him here) or destitute of all but life itself (as we find him at the end of Job chapter 2), he maintained the same character and relationship with God. In both circumstances, God was in control. Job did not experience anything in life that had escaped God's attention. God was confident in Job's character and relationship and chose him to be His champion in this battle with evil.

Reality from a biblical perspective is physical and spiritual; Job lived in both, and we live in both. It is not an either-or choice. One is not more real than the other. The Bible declares that God created the physical world (Gen. 1:1). It had a beginning and is moving toward a conclusion (Rev. 21:1). A personal relationship with the creator God sets biblical Christianity apart from other religions. Virtually every religious perspective other than the Judeo-Christian worldview sees humankind in some form of evolving ascendency. The goal is to be like God (Is. 14:12–14) or to become one with God (Is. 48:11). Neither of these options is Christian or biblical. Though we are separated from God, He desires to have a relationship and oversees the events and conditions of our lives. Jesus even characterizes it as friendship (John 15:15).

The way we live is directly affected by how we define God and the nature of the world in which we live. As the story unfolds, the spiritual drama of eternity is enacted on earth. God and Satan are in a conflict that plays itself out in Job's life. God has chosen him to be the champion of relationship and grace, and He chooses you and me as well. Because of the practical implications, it is important we understand the nature of this conflict, which fortunately has an end, which we read about in Revelation. In the meantime, between its beginning and end, the earth, our physical existence, is the stage for this spiritual drama.

The events of Jesus' life and the cross help us grasp this battle. At the beginning of Jesus' ministry, we see Satan trying to get Jesus to walk away from His commitment to save the world by going to the cross (Matt. 4 and Luke 4). We see Him in the garden entwined with this spiritual conflict, praying for us, praying for His own strength, dripping sweat from His forehead like great drops of blood. All of this is due to the

9

raging spiritual conflict He resolved with, "Your will be done" (Matt. 26:42). No doubt, Satan thought he had won. Jesus was arrested, judicially condemned, beaten, crucified, and buried. You should never lose sight of the fact that God is bigger than the schemes of Satan and the circumstances of life. We can see it at the cross, but can we see it in our lives? When we look back at the cross, we see the entire drama unfold, beginning, middle, and end. When it comes to our own lives, we have a hard time seeing and understanding the present. The past is clouded by our opinions, and the future is unknown. This is the world in which God has placed us, and we must rely on Him.

Though we are separated from God, He has graciously provided for each of us. However, there is an adversary. We need to be careful not to be sucked into Satan's schemes and deceptions. As God's children, we are a part of His eternal plan, not insignificant nobodies. We are His champions. We are a part of His living demonstration for the inhabitants of the heavens and earth to see. We are examples of His love, mercy, and grace. We are a demonstration of His provision for His people. We are a part of this drama. We should be excited, even in difficult places. We are part of His plan. We are to bring glory and praise to God. He explains to Habakkuk at a difficult time, "The glory of the LORD will cover the earth as the waters cover the sea" (Hab. 2:14). God is victorious; Satan is defeated. As we continue in the book of Job, as we live, let us remember the end of the story. Job is faithful; he spoke what was right about God (Job 42:7). We are being perfected (Phil. 1:6). God is victorious!

CHAPTER 2
Tragedy and Worship
Job 1:13–22

In this chapter we will consider the outcome of the discussion and agreement between God and Satan that took place in the last chapter. We see that decisions by the heavenlies have direct impact on the events in our lives. The spiritual is not disconnected from the physical or the eternal from the temporal. The book of Job wastes no time tackling the divergence of man-made religious thought from a biblical understanding of the world in which we live. Broadly put, religious thought offers or creates explanations for the experiences of life. A biblical understanding believes that God reigns. Human thought may attribute the circumstances of life to the alignment of the stars, the time of year we were born, satisfied and unsatisfied spiritual forces, or random chance. Job's experiences and expressions are counterintuitive to human religious thought. However, before we consider the events and ideas of the passage, let us review the ideas from the last chapter.

From the opening scene in heaven and the challenge issued by Satan, we considered three aspects of our spiritual reality that separates biblical thought from other religious thought. The first concept we considered was the fact that individuals fall short of God's standards. The second truth discussed was that both good and evil are personal, not inanimate forces, ends of a spectrum, or parts of a whole. The conflict between God and Satan is lived out on earth. The last aspect of our spiritual reality we explored was the fact God is in control. When we reject God's view of reality, we are adrift in the shifting tides of religious and philosophic theory without meaningful explanation and purpose.

That was not Job's experience because he was God's champion. Job found meaning in life and was able to worship God regardless of his circumstances. Let me encourage you to read Job 1:13–22. In these ten verses, we learn that Job had lost everything. His possessions had been stolen. His children had died. His wife encouraged him to curse God and die. However, Job responded, "Blessed be the name of the Lord" (Job 1:21). With that as the story, let us ask how it was possible for Job to worship God in the midst of such devastating tragedy. If we can answer that question, we will be able to apply the same answer to our lives.

We have lived long enough to know that tragedy is part of everyone's life. None of us is exempt from its invasion into our experiences, possessions, or relationships. Whether it is expected or unexpected, we are adrift in mind-numbing circumstances that seem overwhelming.

Satan's assertion that it is easy to live life claiming to love God when everything is going well is accurate enough. We love it when life is stable, predictable, and adequate, preferably abundant. However, that has not been and is not the reality for most Christians. Today, most Christians around the world live in difficult circumstances on a daily basis. They fear hostile armed forces and worry about food. Those of us who have not really experienced much hardship have much to learn from Job. I believe certain aspects of Job's relationship with God enabled him to worship in spite of the suffering due to the tragic loss of family and his earthly possessions. The first point is that Job knew how to worship God before he faced this head-spinning, gut-wrenching, seemingly senseless loss. Our ability to worship God cannot depend on the circumstances.

12

When tragedy strikes, worshiping God tends not to be the first response for most people, even many who would claim to be a part of God's kingdom. Because we human beings tend to be self-centered and self-serving, we tend to think and respond to life's circumstances as though it were all about us. It is not. What Job experienced had nothing to do with him. As we reviewed earlier, this was about God's character. Job was the main character in a grand and eternal demonstration of God's grace, mercy, and love. He was God's champion. He carried God's reputation in this battle. Satan did not believe there was depth to Job's relationship with God and wanted to prove that people would not serve God unless they got something out of it.

The fact was that Job worshiped God because He was worthy of worship. It was an engrained part of who Job was. Referencing the loss of Job's children in verse 13 takes us back to verse 5. It tells us that Job regularly made sacrifice for his children. Some interpret his actions in such a way as to accuse him of fear, worry, or other misguided attitudes. However, that doesn't sound like a guy God could count on in a challenge with Satan. I would suggest such a notion is at odds with the joint opinion of God and Satan. They agreed Job was a man of character who worshiped God; the point of disagreement revolved around why Job worshiped God. Satan believed it was due to God's blessing and protection; God believed it was due to the relationship He had with Job.

Consistent with this view, there is the opinion that Job was a priest of the Most High God. This would suggest that Job had an understanding of the atoning sacrifice before the Law was given through Moses. In Leviticus 16, we find a description of the annual sacrifice for the sins committed by God's people, Israel. Hebrews 9:17 expands our understanding; there we learn this sacrifice is for sins "committed in ignorance." Because of Job's relationship with God, he understood God was merciful and gracious. God had made a provision for sin whether intentional or unintentional. Job was the leader of his family. He stood in the spiritual gap for his children. He knew how to worship God. As priest, he made sacrifice for the sins committed in ignorance by his children and family.

Some other important verses speak about our relationship with God. David, a man after God's own heart (1 Sam. 13:14; Acts 13:22), knew the importance of relying on God. He expressed his dependence in Psalm 37:3–5. He used the words "trusting," "delighting," and "committing," relational words. David also knew God was gracious and forgiving. Solomon, David's son, knew the importance of this relationship. In Proverbs 3:5–6, he spoke of trusting in the Lord. He knew the importance of depending on God and allowing Him to direct. Micah also knew God expected us to walk humbly with Him (Mic. 6:8). It should not be a surprise that Job walked with God and lived a life in relationship with Him. He knew how to worship God long before his life unraveled by what appeared to be the unfortunate circumstances of life. We need that kind of relationship with God before the challenges.

The next quality in Job's life that enabled him to worship in spite of personal tragedy was his understanding of ownership. He knew he was a steward, not an owner. What he had was not his; he was entrusted to care for what God had provided him. This characteristic and the next two come from Job's response in verse 21. It begins with a phrase that recognizes he came into the world with nothing and will leave the same way. He declares, "The Lord gives and the Lord takes away." When we understand we are not the owners of what we have, loss has a very different impact on our lives. While it might be gone, we have not lost it. It was never ours; it was a trust from God. This concept is true for material possessions, personal relationships, jobs, even health. Our expectations and sense of ownership cause us to react possessively rather than worship the owner of all things.

Paul gave Timothy some instructions regarding the things of this world in 1 Timothy 6:7–10. The short version of Paul's direction is to be content with food and covering. He made this observation based on the same understanding Job had; he had come into the world with nothing and was leaving with nothing. In this passage, Paul declared that the love of worldly wealth was the root of all kinds of evil. It created temptation, destruction, and grief. It even caused people to wander away from the faith. Do we take Paul's words seriously? Have we entangled ourselves? A time of loss will reveal our hearts' commitments. Jesus said we could serve only one master (Matt. 6:24). For most of us, our contentment level requires way more than food and covering.

Ananias and Sapphira experienced the consequences of not living out their stewardship. We learn of their poor behavior in Acts 5. There was a financial crisis in Jerusalem, and some were selling what they had and giving the proceeds to the church to help provide the basic needs of others. They of course were recognized for their generosity, and Ananias and Sapphira wanted in on the accolades. They had property they could sell and decided to give some of what they received and keep some. The problem arose because they declared they had given it all. Peter told them that the property was theirs. When they sold it, the money was theirs. They had the freedom to do with it as they chose. However, when they decided to take credit for doing something they had not done, they were lying to the Holy Spirit and were no longer being good stewards of what God had entrusted to their care. They chose to take personal glory, and it cost them their lives. When we mishandle our stewardship and misrepresent our actions to God, it does not create an environment conducive to worship. Stewards know how to worship God, the giver of all things. They are not entangled by the things they have. They recognize His grace and can bask in His love. They enjoy all He has provided without expectations.

Jesus lived this truth. John 1:1–3 tells us that Jesus was always with the Father and that He created everything. A few verses later (John 1:14), we are told Jesus became flesh, the eternal Word became human. Paul gives us more detail in Philippians 2. Jesus did not hold onto what was rightfully His. He chose to become a man, setting aside what He had as God. He was even willing to die on the cross. He was a steward of our salvation. It was for the joy of relationship with us that He died in our place (Heb. 12:2). Are we good stewards, good worshipers?

The third truth that enables Job to worship was about control. He understood he was not in control; God was. He declared the Lord gave and the Lord took away. He did not believe in random chaos. He saw life as under the purview of God. Have you ever asked someone, "How are you doing?" After they responded, "Okay under the circumstances," did you want to reply, "What are you doing under those?" Job didn't believe he was under the circumstances; he believed he was under God's supervision. God taught Jeremiah this lesson in an interesting way. He sent him down to the potter (Jer. 18:1–6), where he learned about the decision making of the one fashioning the clay. Job, a long time before Jeremiah, believed his experiences were at the hand of God.

Too many people approach this seemingly difficult issue with an either-or mentality when Scripture seems to present it as a both-and issue. I remember when we discussed this in my seminary class. Dr. Saucy drew a line down the middle of the board and on either side wrote the two positions, free will and sovereignty. He turned to the class and said, "The further you wander from the line, the closer you move toward heresy." Biblical truth is not found in pushing one side or the other. Any two-bit god can manipulate and control or throw up his hands and say, "Whatever." It takes a real God, the God of heaven and earth, to empower our choices for better or worse and still accomplish His will through us. That is the God of Job.

While the book of Job is revealing the character and nature of God, some men and women in the Bible understood and accepted God's active decision making in their lives while acknowledging their personal responsibility. One was Hannah, Samuel's mother. In the first chapter of 1 Samuel, Hannah prayed for a son. At first the priest chided, her but after a brief conversation he blessed her. At the end of the chapter, Samuel was being dedicated and given back to the Lord. Chapter 2 opened with a prayer of thanksgiving by

Hannah. Verses 6 through 8 of that chapter spoke to God's active superintendence of life. Hannah understood well the God she knew. She did not believe that Samuel was the result of random choice but a gift from the God she worshiped. When we have this big picture view of God, we can worship regardless of the circumstances.

Psalm 104 is a celebration of God's active involvement in the activities on earth. David tells us that God participated in the very formation of our lives inside our mothers (Ps. 139:13). Jesus tells us that God knows the number of hairs on our heads (Matt. 10:30). When we see life as a gift from God with whom we have a gracious and compassionate relationship, we can worship. When we see God as an active, caring agent in our lives, we can worship. When we know the God who "is" rather than the God we want Him to be, we can truly worship. Job could worship through the experience of loss because he had already developed a relationship with God. He could worship because he understood he was a steward, not an owner, of things he had. He could worship because he accepted God's superintendence of his life.

The last point regarding Job's ability to worship is based on his statement. Even in the center of his personal storm he could bless, honor, and worship God. Job walked by faith, not by sight. His response came from what he knew and had experienced already with God. Job's ability to worship was a flesh-and-blood example of faith. Paul tells us in 2 Corinthians 5:17, "we walk by faith, not by sight." This is in the middle of his explaining the implication of our living in temporal bodies that have eternal, spiritual futures. Our relationship with God regarding the future is premised on our convictions about things we cannot see. The book of Hebrews (11:1) declares, "Faith is the assurance of things hoped for, the conviction [evidence] of things not seen."

This life-transforming faith is not a relative of wishful thinking. It is not connected to something that may or may not happen; it is anchored in the same certainty of creation. God said, "Let there be light and there was light" (Gen. 1:5).

It is fastened to the same unwavering expectation Habakkuk had when he penned the words "The righteous will live by his faith" (Hab. 2:4). Habakkuk was not happy about the impending judgment of God. Jerusalem was about to be destroyed by Babylon. In spite of his object to God's intentions, Habakkuk was certain it would happen. He, like Job before him, knew that destruction and devastation was not the whole story, nor would it be the end of the story. By faith, Habakkuk rested in the God he knew. By faith, Job could worship God.

When our focus is on God, we are not confused about worship or drawn out of His presence. We do not have mixed feelings. Job's faith rested securely on the God he knew. As a result of his faith-based relationship with God, he could worship even when tragedy had engulfed all he had. He was not depending on the accomplishment of his actions or the accumulation of his possessions but a relationship with the eternal, compassionate God he knew.

Job was a man on whom God was willing to stake his reputation. God had a relationship with Job and knew he had a worshiper's heart. God knew that Job considered all he had as gifts rather than possessions and that Job lived in submission, allowing God to be God. God knew Job was a man of faith who was properly focused on the things above (Col. 3:1).

Job had learned the truth written by the psalmist in Psalm 73:25 and 28, "Whom have I in heaven but you? And besides You, I desire nothing on earth." He continued a few verses later, "But as for me, the nearness of God is my good, I have made the Lord God my refuge, that I may tell of all Your works." For most people, the things of this earth keep us from such a confident understanding of who God is. We waver when it comes to possessions or family. We have second thoughts when we are challenged by health or rejection. But Job did not; he could worship the God he knew, secure in his relationship with God.

Maybe the experience of Job ran through the mind of Horatio Spafford when he received the telegram from his wife, or as he stood on the deck in the place of a sunken ship, or after he returned to his cabin. We know Job shared a common experience as expressed in the words he penned.

When peace, like a river, attendeth my way,

When sorrow like sea billow roll

Whatever my lot,

Thou hast taught me to say,

It is well, it is well with my soul.

These words are beautifully sung, but have we learned the capacity to sing them with Horatio or Job?

CHAPTER 3
The Challenge Continues
Job 2:1–10

In the first chapter, we asked about the nature of reality and made observations about the world in which we live. In the second chapter, we saw massive tragedy poured out in the life of Job. Because difficulties are a common experience, we asked, "How do we worship in the midst of tragedy?" We answered that question with four observations about Job. First, he already knew how to worship because it was a part of his life. Whether it was the evening before or that morning, he would have made sacrifice to the God he knew because he was rejoicing in his God. He was asking for forgiveness and enjoying the relationship with the God he loved and who loved him. Satan then poured chaos into his life, but Job could worship in the midst of trials because he already knew how.

Second, he understood he was only a steward of his stuff. It was not his, and ours is not ours, but losing it makes us angry. We think we have a right to it, but we are just stewards of what God entrusts to our care.

Third, Job accepted God's control. When we think we are in control and the world cycles out of order, we are left in a quagmire of confusion. Life always has its struggles, so when we accept the fact that God is in control, we can rest in the faith that somebody who cares knows what is happening.

The last characteristic that enabled Job to worship was his walk of faith. He did not know what was happening or why it was happening, and that is often the reality of our experience; we are frequently at a loss for answers and do not understand. Nevertheless, by faith Job bowed down, worshiped, and declared his hope in the God he knew. "The Lord gave and the Lord has taken away. Blessed be the name of the Lord" (Job 1:21b). God is gracious and loving. He provides for us. Let us move to Job chapter 2 and a second attack on Job.

We would think—foolish us—that Satan had it figured out. God knew what He was doing, and He was right. However, we human beings often find ourselves on the wrong side of the eternal, spiritual perspective (read Job 2:1–10). This is an amazing picture of God's grace, mercy, power, and investment in the lives of his people and also a picture of the dependence of one who loved God and who was persuaded God was good and loved him. The truths in these verses will probably push us outside our comfort zones.

We did not deal much with Satan in the conflict of chapter 1. As we come to round two, we will see it can get much worse and even worse still when we move to Job 3. In our current text, we should ask, "What is the nature of our spiritual battle?" What takes place in this spiritual arena that we discussed in the first chapter? There, we explored that we have an adversary evidenced by the conflict between God and Satan. What is the nature of this spiritual conflict? How does it operate? We will answer these questions as we work through the first ten verses of chapter 2.

The first thing we know, because we may have experienced it, is that Satan is persistent and potentially progressive in battle. Satan does not give up; he does not take no for an answer, and he will be persistent in the challenges of our lives. Sometimes his persistence may be very immediate, while other times there could be significant intervals between them. When it comes to the battle of eternity, Satan will be relentless;

it may get worse. God will determine if you can handle Satan taking it up a notch. Satan does not play fair. He understands the past and is living in the present, but he does not know the future. He should. God has told him. He is on the losing end of this. He has had a lot of opportunity to observe humanity. He knows how we tick, so he will be persistent in his efforts to wear us down.

In regard to Job, Satan challenged God by complaining that He had protected him, but if God took away all Job's possessions, he would curse God to His face. God said, "Oh, really!" All the stuff disappeared. Nevertheless, Job maintained his integrity, and God was proven right. Satan flat out ignored this and instead proceeded with additional accusations. However, God knew what He was doing. Job would maintain his uprightness, and God would be vindicated again. Satan was wrong. Praise God! Our relationship with God gives us a foundation and a security in which we can rest with certainty, as did Job.

Too many people do not seem to believe this. I have read several commentaries and books as well as heard people comment on Job. It is common to accuse Job of two things. First, he is accused of being a fearful man. They say he was making regular sacrifice because he was afraid that his children had committed sin, that something had gone wrong, that something bad might happen. Second, he is accused of arrogance. Out of his arrogance he was making sacrifices for everybody else because he was above it all. Out of his arrogance he later demanded to meet with God. These accusers, like his friends we will meet later, concluded he got what he deserved or at least opened the door due to his poor character.

I have a problem with either assertion and would like to believe you do too. At face value, it is contrary to a biblical view of grace and what the text says. What did God ask? "Have you considered my servant Job? There is no one like him on the earth." This is followed by a description of what that means, "a blameless and upright man, fearing God and turning away from evil." If God says someone is blameless and upright, be very careful when you listen to people with a different opinion. It is not wise to hold opinions contrary to God's. God is always right; they will be wrong. Later, we will learn they are doing exactly what Job's accusers did when we look at the interaction with his friends. They try to come up with some reason why God allowed this man to suffer. If he was arrogant, they claim he deserved to suffer. If he was fearful, he brought it on himself. He sinned—too bad, he had it coming. It is not God's opinion at the beginning of the book (Job 1:8), nor is it God's opinion at the end of the book (Job 42:7). It is important, as we look at Satan's participation in this conflict, that we remember God's perspective.

Let us remember Satan will be persistent and possibly progressive in his attacks. I offer some examples. The first has no proof other than our common humanity. It was Eve's decision to eat the fruit. I do not think she took the fruit off the tree the first time the Serpent pointed out it was good-looking fruit. Maybe she did, but from the perspective of her humanity and walking with God, he probably had to wear her down. It seems reasonable there were multiple conversations over an extended time. Obviously, this is not in Scripture, but that is how we tick. Eve was human and walked with God in the cool of the evening. Typically, it often takes persistence for contrary voices to prevail.

The second example is Jesus in Matthew 4. There are three separate temptations. Jesus is tempted by Satan to sin, to take a shortcut, to avoid the cross. Each temptation was progressive in terms of what Jesus was challenged to do. At first He was asked to turn a stone to bread because He was hungry. In the end, He was urged to jump off a tower and have the angels show up. This was far more serious. In 1 Peter 5:8, we learn "Your adversary, the devil, prowls around like a roaring lion, seeking someone to devour." The spiritual battle we face is persistent. Peter rightly underscores the importance of prayer, which also needs to be persistent.

The second perspective I offer regarding the nature of our spiritual battle is a reminder that it is not about us but rather about God's glory, grace, and character. We are bit players in a small slice of history, not the story. The spiritual battle really has nothing to do with us. The big picture story in the book of Job had nothing to do with Job. He was a righteous man in pursuit of his relationship with God. This was a direct attack on God. Satan was simply trying to use Job as his agent. His goal was to get Job to deny God and demonstrate the failure of God's grace and love. He did not care about Job's health, possessions, or relationships; he was looking to attack God. In our conflicts and spiritual battles, we must remember the whole point of the conflict from Satan's perspective was an attack on God. He wants us to be angry, to steal, to be immoral. He doesn't care about us. He wants us to deny the God who changed and altered our characters by the finished work of the cross. He wants us to lose credibility and impact in the lives of those around us. Satan can then stand and say, "I told you you were a loser. No one is going to believe you when you talk about Jesus. What makes you think you're so good?" Heard any of these taunts? Satan is good with his lines, and he keeps repeating them because they work. But remember it is an attack on God, on His character, provision, and decision to say, "You are my child." Satan is the accuser of the brethren (Rev. 10:12). He is still standing in heaven telling God, "You made a mistake with that one." He continues to look for opportunity to attack God through His people.

Let us consider Isaiah 14:12–14, which will give us additional insight into Satan's plans. In context, this passage deals with God's judgment on one of the current kings. Yet this passage was interpreted as a reference to Satan even by ancient Jewish commentators. Here are Satan's goals, his "I wills":

> How you have fallen from heaven, O star of the morning, son of the dawn! You have been cut down to the earth, you who have weakened the nations! But you said in your heart, "I will ascend to heaven; I will raise my throne above the stars of God, and I will sit on the mount of assembly in the recesses of the north. I will

ascend above the heights of the clouds; I will
make my self like the Most High."

Satan has not changed his goals. When we find ourselves in
the midst of spiritual conflict, it is God who is under attack, not
us. We are merely the agents in this spiritual conflict working
itself out in the physical realities where we live.

The third reality of spiritual conflict comes in verses 3
through 8. We learn here the battle exists under God's control.
We know this because God says He is the decision maker.
Verses 6 through 8 say,

> So the Lord said to Satan, "Behold, he is in your
> power, only spare his life." then Satan went out
> from the presence of the Lord and smote Job
> with sore boils from the sole of his foot to the
> crown of his head. And he took a potsherd to
> scrape himself while he was sitting among the
> ashes.

Satan left God and inflicted significant bodily harm on Job.
Without God's permission, Satan was powerless to attack Job,
either his possessions in the earlier attack or his person here.

If we look back to verse 3, we see an interesting aspect of
this truth. God says regarding Job's character, "And he still
holds fast his integrity, although you incited Me against him
to ruin him without cause." I understand there is a debate
regarding what God does, what Satan does, and how we are
a part of that conflict. Let me give an example of why this is a
debate. Consider 1 Chronicles 21:1, in which David was king,
and things were going reasonably well. David wanted to build
a temple, but God said no because he was a man of bloodshed.
Eventually, David had a census taken, and there was judgment
because of his action. The verse reads, "Then Satan stood up
against Israel and moved David to number Israel." God had
told David not to number Israel; if he did, there would be
judgment. We now need to consider 2 Samuel 24:1, in which
the same situation was discussed. "Now again the anger of the

Lord burned against Israel, and it incited David against them to say, 'Go, number Israel and Judah.'" In 2 Samuel we learn God did it; 1 Chronicles says Satan did it. Conflict on. These two accounts give differing perspectives regarding what took place in terms of Satan's responsibility, God's sovereignty, David's actions, and the whole scenario of what happened. Sometimes we are confused because we have a hard time believing God may do things we do not consider appropriate. In reality, we always have a hard time understanding why God does what He does because God is God and we are limited.

Let us take an example from Jesus' life. Jesus and his disciples were traveling from city to city and came across a man born blind, an event related in John 9. A disciple asked Jesus, "Is this man blind because of his sin or his parents' sin?" One of those choices would have been the common cultural understanding of the day; if you suffered a wrong, it was because God was punishing you for your sin. There was a direct correlation between poor situations or circumstances and behavior. The disciples expressed this direct connection in their thinking, and people today also make this connection. However, Jesus responded to the disciple, "Neither, not this man's sin, not his parents' sin." He said God had done it for His own glory. We struggle emotionally with that fact. We do not allow for the idea God would cause a person to be born blind merely for His own glory.

Let me give some more examples in which we emotionally struggle with the nature and character of who God is and how He acts. God rejected Saul as king and told Samuel He wanted him to anoint a new king (1 Sam. 16). Samuel responded that Saul would not let him live that long if he knew he was going to anoint a king. God told him it would not be a problem. "Tell Saul if you are asked, that you are going to make sacrifice and then anoint a king." Consider Psalm 119:75: "I know, O Lord, that Your judgments are righteous, and that in faithfulness You have afflicted me." When we normally read such passages, we read right over these verses. We never stop and give them much thought regarding God's interaction in our lives and what God does. We resist the notion that God might "afflict" us. Isaiah 45:7 says, "The One forming light and creating darkness, causing well-being and creating calamity; I am the Lord who does all these." God takes personal, direct responsibility. This does not stop the debate we discussed with David numbering Israel. Satan was an active participant, and God's anger obviously motivated it. Nevertheless, let us not put God in our sterile box of limited thinking because our humanity is uncomfortable with His sovereignty.

We also have an interesting story in 2 Chronicles 18. King Ahab was one of many evil kings in Israel; he got special mention for being particularly bad. Jehoshaphat, king of Judah, came to visit, and they discussed going to war. Ahab wanted to fight the Assyrian king and invited Jehoshaphat to join him. In reply, Jehoshaphat said that sounded good, they should fight. Jehoshaphat asked if there was a prophet of the Lord; he wanted to ask if they should fight and if they would have success. He was seeking wisdom and God's perspective in this venture. Ahab said there was, but the prophet did not like him. He drew that conclusion because he had prophesied his doom. Micaiah, a prophet of the Lord, was called. He told them to fight and the Lord would prosper their effort. Ahab challenged him to tell the truth. So Micaiah agreed and told him he saw sheep scattered on the hills of Israel. Additionally, he told him he was going to die. Ahab told Jehoshaphat he had known the prophet would prophecy against him. Micaiah declared the words of the Lord and spoke of a heavenly vision where Ahab's defeat and death were being discussed.

> Then a spirit came forward and stood before the Lord and said, "I will entice him." And the Lord said to him, "How?" He said, "I will go and be a deceiving spirit in the mouth of all his prophets." Then He said, "You are to entice him and prevail also. Go and do so." (2 Chron. 18:20, 21)

God told a spirit under His control to go be a deceiving spirit in the mouth of Ahab's prophets. This is not in the comfort zone of our thinking about God.

These verses are God's declarations about Himself, so when we look at Job, we need to realize, regardless of our preconceived ideas about God's appropriate behavior, He does not say the Devil made Him do it. If God does not say it, neither can we. Whatever our understanding is, Satan is still a roaring lion (1 Pet. 5:8). He is still seeking whom he can devour, still engaged in conflict. He encouraged Eve, inspired David, and motivated Peter. Nevertheless, God is still in control. We need to understand the nature of this conflict in Job's life. Later, we will need to ponder if our struggle with who God is and how He acts might cause us to side with Job's friends. It will help bring meaning to the circumstances we may face.

Let us turn to the fourth truth regarding spiritual battles. We have seen Satan is persistent; his attack is on God, but the conflict exists under God's control. The fourth truth is that Satan uses human agency. In Job 2:9, Job's wife said, "Curse God and die!" Satan does not act alone; he uses people and circumstances. In Job's life it was armies, nature, family, health, and friends. In this situation and in the nature of spiritual conflict, he continues to use all these. It is not just "bad" people, our enemies, or the faceless masses; it is just as likely those close to us. We should expect and not be surprised to see human agency in the spiritual conflict of heaven.

Adam did not pick the fruit; Eve brought it to him, but Adam was still responsible for his choice to eat it. The Serpent did not talk with Adam. If he did, it was not recorded in Scripture. We do not know if it was the first piece Eve ate. The exchange between Adam and Eve could have happened later. She may have been enjoying the fruit and talking to Adam about how good it was. Finally, Adam gave in. Human agency was used to motivate Adam to sin.

We know human agency was also used in Jesus' life. When He was headed to the cross, Peter told Him he did not need to die. Jesus responded to the real source, "Get behind me

Satan" (Matt. 16:23). He understood who motivated this attack on God's plan. So in our own lives, there may be times when Satan will use friends, even close friends like Peter, family, like Eve, to challenge what God is doing. Satan's goal is for us to deny the God we love and who loves us.

The book of 1 Peter seems to be an appropriate place to conclude our thoughts. Jesus told Peter at the Last Supper that Satan desired to sift him (Luke 22:31). Peter said that everyone else might fall away but he would not; Peter was willing to die with Jesus. Peter at that point did not understand the nature of the conflict, but Jesus did; 1 Peter 1:6–9 reads,

> In this you greatly rejoice, even though now for a little while, if necessary, you have been distressed by various trials, so that the proof of your faith, being more precious than gold which is perishable, even though tested by fire, may be found to result in praise and glory and honor at the revelation of Jesus Christ; and though you have not seen Him, you love Him, and though you do not see Him now, but believe in Him, you greatly rejoice with joy inexpressible and full of glory, obtaining as the outcome of your faith the salvation of your souls.

There is something more important than our comfort. Job understood, and we need to understand. We too will be agents, actors, in this eternal conflict between Satan and God. Satan will be persistent in his attacks on God, but the attacks are under God's control. Satan may well use those around us, but God will be glorified. Peter learned the lesson. He denied Jesus at the trial but later saw the Spirit poured out at Pentecost; he learned that the glory of God was the end of the process. When we do not believe the glory of God is the goal, the present circumstances will overwhelm us.

CHAPTER 4

Comforters

Job 2:11–13

It would be good to read verses 11–13 of Job chapter 3. They discuss Job's friends coming to comfort him. These three verses are amazing. Just sitting and saying nothing for seven days is not in most people's experience. There are significant truths God wants us to know. However, let us review the ideas of the last chapter, in which we explored the nature of the spiritual battle we are involved in. At one level, we live in a physical, tangible world. However, we are also engaged in a spiritual dimension. First, we considered that Satan is persistent and progressive in his attacks in our lives. Second, the spiritual battle is about spiritual issues. They are not about you and me; they are not about the events or circumstances of our physical lives. They are conflict between God and Satan, between good and evil. In Job's experience, it was an attack on God's character, His relationship with humanity, and grace. We will lose spiritual perspective if we think it is about us.

Third, all life and its circumstances exist under God's control. The world has not spun out of order into chaos. God is not in heaven wringing His hands wondering what He is going to do next. God is still God. The last concept we explored was that Satan uses people, sometimes those closest to us.

Because of this, it can be very challenging to maintain our understanding that it is about God and not about us.

In these last three verses of Job chapter 2, we find Job has lost everything and was sitting in the dust, in excruciating physical and emotional agony from the top of his head to the soles of his feet. Some who cared about him came to comfort him. In this chapter we will talk about his three friends, Eliphaz, Bildad, and Zophar. They take a lot of grief for being lousy comforters, just as Job takes grief for failing (see Appendix A). However, let us remember what God said to Satan: "Have you considered my servant Job, a blameless and upright man?" In God's analysis, Job was blameless and upright; in the end, God declares Job spoke what was right about Him. So let's not find fault with Job; it is not a good thing to disagree with God.

Being called "poor comforters" seems a little harsh for those willing to leave the comfort of their homes, travel a considerable distance, and sit on the ground in the dust for seven days. While they may not have accomplished "their" goal, I think they did a pretty good job of demonstrating the skills of bringing comfort to the hurting. So before we consider how we can comfort the suffering, let us take some time to learn a little about his friends. I do not believe they failed in the comfort department; they were good comforters for at least a week.

We have lessons to learn from Job's three friends, but who are they? They have a major role in the balance of the book of Job, most of which is a conversation between these three and Job. The short and really accurate answer about these three is we do not really know. However, one of the names shows up in genealogical lists in Genesis. More helpful is the tag to his name, which gives us some idea of where he might have lived. The name Eliphaz is mentioned several times in Genesis 36. He is a son of Esau, the son of Isaac, the son of Abraham. We also learn in that chapter that Teman was the oldest son of Eliphaz. It is believed that the city or the area of Teman, which could have been founded and named after the oldest son, is southeast of the Dead Sea, and it is mentioned several times by various prophets. Jeremiah asks, "Is there no wisdom in Teman?" (Jer. 49:7). This is in the context of judgment upon Esau. The area is to the south of Israel. Other prophets declare God's judgment on Teman. Ezekiel (25:13), Amos (1:12), Obadiah (verse 9), and Habakkuk (3:3) speak specifically about Teman. We are not sure if it is the same person. Due to the lack of specific timing of these events, it leaves us uncertain as to any connection.

Bildad and Zophar are not mentioned elsewhere in the Bible, nor are the cities or areas referenced. Some believe that Bildad, the Shuhite, might be from the city of Shua. It is possible this city was in the southwest area of what would become Israel and later Judah. It is speculated that the city or area in which Zophar lived might be in northwest Israel. Given that each could have traveled some distance to visit Job for an extended period, they could have been wealthy, influential members of their communities.

While they did not understand the spiritual nature of the problem or the relational nature of God, their actions are instructive for us today. Some of us need God's comfort and mercy, the engaging touch of God's love and grace because of what we are experiencing. We need to be comforted, and we need to comfort others with the lessons we have learned (2 Cor. 1:3–4). These verses are relevant to our lives. Our hearts tell us at times that others are in pain and in need of our comfort. However, our minds will tell us, *You can't do that. You don't know how.* So in this chapter about Job's friends, I want you to learn some tools for bringing comfort to hurting hearts.

The first lesson we can learn about comforting the suffering is that we can do it with our presence. We physically, personally need to show up. It is eye to eye that they can see our hearts and know we are sharing their suffering. It takes our presence. Cards are great, phone calls are great, and social media is great, and in our worlds they might even be necessary. In spite of the shrinking nature of our world and exploding advancements in technology, it can be difficult to leave everything and show up elsewhere on short notice. Regardless, Job's friends agreed to visit Job, to make the effort to see him in person. They made a commitment to touch Job's hurting life. Their presence brought comfort, and our presence might bring comfort today.

I remember learning this concept from one of my church members. He told me we needed to visit a woman in the hospital, so we traveled the little distance involved. Our presence brought comfort in a difficult situation. My wife helps me from time to time with similar encouragement, "We need to visit." Our presence, our being with hurt hearts brings comfort.

Jesus understood this concept and shared it with us in John 14. He and His disciples were sharing a meal in the Upper Room when Jesus was only hours from the cross. While he had told the disciples He was going to die, they did not understand what He had been telling them. At the beginning of the chapter, Jesus shared with them some significant truths to bring comfort to their hearts and our hearts. Chapter 14 begins with the words, "Do not let your heart be troubled." The words can be easy to say. However, later in the meal Jesus spoke the words of verse 16,

> I will ask the Father and He will give you another Helper [Some translate the word as "Comforter."] that He may be with you forever. That is the spirit of truth that the world cannot receive because it does not see Him or know Him. But you know Him because He abides with you and will be in you.

The Spirit of God is the abiding presence of Jesus in our hearts. He told them and us He will be with us. They were about to experience the loss of His physical presence. In that eventuality, they were going to need Him with them, just as we do. In His physical absence, the need would increase. He was making them a promise; He was committed to being with them no matter what the future held. This is not just for them; it is also for us. We need His presence as desperately as did the disciples. We too need the comfort His presence brings, and in the same way our presence brings comfort to those around us who are hurting. He comforts us with His presence so we can comfort others (2 Cor. 1:4). Our presence will speak comfort to those who are suffering.

The second point this text illustrates about comfort when Job's friends came to him is the importance of taking appropriate action. Actions speak; they tell a story. They can comfort the hurting. They tore their clothes and threw dirt in the air. Their actions were appropriate for their culture, but they would not be appropriate today. We might send a card or bring a meal. Many churches are really good at seeing what would bring comfort to hurting families. Often they provide meals whether on the loss or the hospitalization of a loved one. Sometimes it may be cutting the grass or pruning the roses. Our actions speak volumes about our compassion and caring, so it is important that we use relevant actions to speak comfort to the hurting. If I am hurting and you show up tearing your robe and throwing dirt in the air, don't be surprised if I want you gone. While comfort may be your intention, inappropriate actions will contribute to the heartache and pain. Adding dirt to my living environment is not going to cause the warm fuzzies that might be intended. Our actions speak, so let them speak comfort.

In our culture a card will speak. It says I am thinking of you and about what is happening in your life. It says I took the time; I made the investment to express my heart for your well-being. It may express I am praying for your need. These actions speak comfort to many. However, let us be careful and thoughtful about the wording of those cards. I have known those who have expressed that receiving a card was comforting, but reading it was not. Some of us are certainly better at doing these things than others, but we can all be more thoughtful, more caring, and more appropriate in our actions, which can bring comfort or contribute to the hurt.

John 11 speaks of the importance of actions that bring comfort. In this chapter, Jesus comes to Bethany, where Lazarus, his friend, had died. I want us to consider verse 35, the shortest verse in the Bible: "Jesus wept." His actions spoke to the entire crowd. Everyone there knew He cared. They all knew he shared their hurting hearts. He knew He was going to raise Lazarus from the dead. At an intellectual level, there was no reason for Him to cry; it was an action contrary to what He knew would be true. Nevertheless, it spoke of His willingness to take the action that would speak comfort to hurting lives. He empathetically entered into their agony. Are we willing to take the necessary actions? His actions spoke loudly to Mary and Martha as well as everyone else who had come to comfort them. The crowd responded to Jesus' action with, "See how much He loved him" (John 11:36). Because our actions speak, it is important to understand what they say. We should do the things that speak comfort to those who are hurting.

One of God's gifts to the church is mercy (Rom. 12:8). Those with this gift have a God-given insight into the emotional dynamic of what is happening in people's lives. They also understand and have an amazing capacity to express God's compassion and care. They just seem to know how to bring comfort and encouragement to hurting hearts. I really praise God for those with this gift because that is not me. It is hard for some of us to develop the skills and understanding of how to bring comfort in times of need. We can learn from those with the gift.

We bring comfort with our presence and our actions. Job's friends saw the need in his life. They altered their lives to spend time with him. They did what they knew would speak of their concern and compassion. They agreed together, they showed up, and they identified with Job's pain. They also sat in silence for seven days, not saying a word. Hopefully, this will give us an achievable task. Our silence speaks comfort.

Probably all readers have experienced heartaches, troubles, the loss of loved ones, or some other suffering in their lives and have probably also experienced having Romans 8:28 thrown at them by someone who thought he or she was well intentioned: "All things work together for good for those who love God." Sometimes it gets rephrased, "Everything has a purpose." You may share my observation that people do not want to hear about silver linings either. When we are confronted by such thoughtless statements, we tend not to respond well. We want to know what their experiences were that made them experts or made them God. We smile and say we understand, but deep down we want to do a smackdown right on the spot. Words do not necessarily speak comfort, and these words are almost guaranteed to fail in their intended task. Silence would have been a much better communicator. An empathetic expression and a hug would have spoken effectively without words. Sometimes we are uncomfortable visiting someone who is hurting or grieving because we do not know what to say. The example of Job's friends should help us out of that dilemma. Do not say anything! Let your silence speak. Your presence will bring the comfort needed. Do what Jesus did; cry with them. Tell them you love them or are there for them if you have to say something.

When the person grieving or suffering is struggling with how to express pain, it is unlikely we will have the proper words to express comfort. Their raw emotional states do not need unnecessary auditory stimulation. Their struggles are overwhelming and drown out most of what is happening and being said around them. They are struggling just to maintain some level of sociability. They really want to withdraw, to hide, and to pretend it is not so. They are physically, mentally, and spiritually stretched; they are distraught and hurting because of the circumstances. They do not need to deal with the barrage of words some feel compelled to express.

The hurting need someone to understand and care. They benefit from those who bring comfort with their presence and silence, which will say they are willing to enter into the pain and care enough to be there. Proverbs 17:28 is instructive: "Even a fool, when he keeps silent, is considered wise; when he closes his lips, he is considered prudent." A related verse that should cause us to pause before we speak is Proverbs 18:2: "A fool does not delight in understanding, but only in revealing his own mind." Too often those who think they have something to say are simply demonstrating their lack of understanding. They could have prevented their foolish behavior by being silent.

We can all improve our compassion for others and their opinion of us by not speaking. Silence can communicate things we do not know how to express and will often make us look better in the eyes of others. Do not miss an opportunity to be silent and communicate well.

Romans 8:26 speaks to compassion without words. The Spirit communicates without words, and we should reflect on it before we so readily jump to verse 28. "In the same way the Spirit also helps our weakness; for we do not know how to pray as we should, but the Spirit Himself intercedes for us with groanings too deep for words." Communication can occur without words. Regarding our spiritual condition and the needs of our lives, the Spirit does not use words to express the need. Requests are not formulated using verbal expression. Our divine Intercessor does not use words to communicate our needs, He uses groanings. There are times that words fail to capture the appropriate expressions of our hearts. In those circumstances, silence is a better choice.

Proverbs 10:19 gives us proper warning. "When there are many words, transgression is unavoidable, but he who restrains his lips is wise." We are familiar with the idea, "Open mouth and insert foot." The verse tells us that when we have our mouths open, our feet slip right in. The idea that silence will bring comfort is consistent with many passages in Scripture.

Since we live in God's world, it is important to comfort those around us. We should express God's heart of compassion and care to those in need. We do that with our presence. We do that with the culturally appropriate actions. We do that with our silence. Jesus models this for us in John 11. As previously referenced, this is the story of raising Lazarus from the dead. We have already applied verse 35. Jesus knows what He is going to do and could have done it from where He was teaching and healing others. However, knowing the importance of His presence for Mary and Martha, He and the disciples traveled to Bethany. We can tell His presence brought comfort, but it also raised questions. He learned where Lazarus had been buried and went to the tomb. This along with His weeping spoke comfort with the appropriate actions. We notice He spoke only to answer their concerns and questions. They had sent Him word of Lazarus's illness earlier, and His delay certainly raised questions. The most important thing He said was, "Lazarus, come forth" (John 11:43). Jesus brought comfort by His presence and His actions. He was cautious with His words, knowing that silence may be more comforting than words. Jesus identifies with our needs and knows how to bring comfort.

We can bring comfort to hurting lives in need of a touch from God. Job's friends did, and Jesus did for Mary and Martha. Are you willing? You can do it with your presence. You can take the necessary actions. You may wisely keep silent.

CHAPTER 5

Let Me Die

Job 3:1–26

Have you considered the chapter title? I have the feeling there are more than a few who have been down that road to the place where circumstances, frustrations, anger, upset, or lack of understanding have conspired to push them over the edge. Some reading this may have had such thoughts, and it may have appeared the short route to the best solution. One can think, "Get me out of here; life is too hard." On the surface, that makes it really tough for this chapter to be encouraging and uplifting; walking through the difficulties and frustrations of life is a regular challenge. This is where we find Job, sitting in the middle of his loss and suffering, cursing the day of his birth. He wants the day removed from the calendar and the sun to stop shining on it. Job is not happy with his life and has a significant list of reasons to be upset: wife estranged, children dead, and health and wealth gone.

As we look at a frustrated Job, let us try to treat him fairly by considering the context and ideas we find in Job chapter 3. They should give us a different perspective than our first impressions. It should be one of compassion so we can weep with those who weep. I think some have gotten lost in the details and missed the big picture, so let us remind ourselves of how a distraught Job came to this point of grief despairing of life.

A spiritual drama initiated in the heavens dominated the first two chapters of Job, a conflict between God and Satan implemented in the experiences of Job's life. Satan's every effort was to push Job to the point of denying God and condemning Him for what He had done. God initiated this particular challenge when He asked Satan, "Have you considered My servant Job? There is no one like him on earth" (1:18). Job was a unique individual, a righteous man. Thus, the battle was engaged.

Satan petitioned to have everything taken away from Job, and God said okay. Job's children were killed. His wealth was removed. Job responded, "The Lord has given and the Lord has taken away. Blessed be the name of the Lord" (Job 1:22b). Satan was not satisfied. He went back to God, who again asked, "Have you considered my servant Job?" (Job 2:3). It did not work out the way Satan planned; God won the challenge. Satan responded, "No big deal. Humans will give up everything to keep on living" (2:4 paraphrased). God then told him he could afflict his body; he could do anything he wanted to Job; he just could not kill him. I am sure Satan was delighted with the outcome of his conversation with God.

With glee and an anticipated victory over God, Satan attacked Job with painful boils from the top of his head to the soles of his feet. Job was in constant, grueling, agonizing pain. Every minute of every day was filled with unbearable, unbelievable pain. The story does not tell us how long this lasted, but one thing is certain: a significant amount of time passed. There were no telephones, post offices, computers, or electronic social media. There were no cars, trains, or planes. The sequence of events required time. After Job's horrific experiences, it would have taken time, weeks maybe longer, for the news of these events to have traveled to his friends. It would have taken time for his friends to interact and decide to visit Job and then to meet and travel to Job. Because of the realities of their culture, this would have taken at least several weeks to several months. So we know Job's suffering lasted for an extended period of time.

Before we consider Job's response, let us reflect on the comfort of his friends. In the previous chapter, we asked, "How do we comfort the suffering?" Job was comforted by his friends' presence. They came; they sat. Second, they comforted Job with the appropriate actions, throwing dirt and tearing clothes. The third aspect of their comfort was their silence. They sat with Job for a week, not saying a word. Often, those who are hurting do not want to hear what we have to say; they want and need just our presence. Our silence, as that of Job's friends, will do the talking for us.

To properly understand the story of Job, especially his struggle, we must believe God knew what He was talking about when He called Job a blameless man (Job 1:8) and that his friends really were friends who brought comfort to Job's suffering. Some commentaries claim that Job, at least on some level, deserved what he got (see Appendix A). Some claim it was a change in attitude over the course of his suffering. Others claim it was Job's fears that allowed Satan to attack him. They also contend that his friends were lousy comforters. I cannot accept these conclusions because they do not square with God's claims. So let's continue our study of Job from the perspective that God was correct when He declared Job to be a righteous man (Job 1:8; 2:3) and that Job had spoken what was right about Him (42:7). I believe that from such a perspective we can learn the truths about the life experiences of Job and the God he knew, a God of grace, the God that will satisfy a thirsty heart.

Job's suffering outweighed the comfort. Job said, "Curses, I hate the day I was born" (3:1, paraphrased). He was upset and grieving. He expressed his opinion that if he had to be born, he should have died immediately. He complained he did not have to live (3:11). He was not happy about being received into life and being sustained (3:12). He was not happy about his mother giving him life. Job's declarations challenged his existence in the middle of the chapter. In the last part of the chapter (3:17–

22), he expressed his objection to being alive in light of the magnitude of his suffering. He complained it would be better if he were not alive. In death, there was no pain, just rest. All cultural and positional distinctions such as slave and master simply disappear. Everyone was at peace. So he asked as a common expression of humanity, "Why do I have to suffer? Why do I have to live with this pain?" Job was really good at complaining in this chapter. There are no positive expressions from blameless and upright Job.

While the chapter is overwhelmingly filled with sorrow and despair, we need to see how this section of Scripture is profitable (2 Tim. 3:16). God has seen fit to include it for our instruction and training in righteousness. We conclude, too easily and quickly, that it is wrong to complain. We should have a stiff upper lip and should just deal with it. Big boys don't cry. Let me suggest that God does not share that perspective. Rugged individualism may have worked well to win the West, but it falls short in the spiritual arena. If the body of Christ is a multigifted organism, there needs to be an open and honest exchange between its members. "Rejoicing with those who rejoice and weeping with those who weep" (Rom. 12:15). There is a reason for their weeping, and they should have the arena to express it. If we do not think that weepers have a legitimate complaint, the body will not function very well. God is a God of grace, which is a provision for a need. If we do not allow for the legitimacy of the need, we will miss the depth and breadth of who God is.

We do not need Job's sorrows added to our own. So given the nature of this chapter, here is the question I want us to answer. Are Job's complaints reasonable? He complained about life, birth, and suffering. If Job was an example of endurance or patience (James 5:11) and vindicated by God, we need to look at this chapter, which diverges from the typical conclusions. Some commentaries tell us that Job was being unreasonable, that he was not trusting in God. If any of this is correct, Satan was right and God was wrong in His statements about Job, but that is an unacceptable conclusion. Let us return to the question rather than dismiss it. Are Job's complaints reasonable?

When you finish reading this chapter and set the book down, I want you to walk away firmly convinced that the answer is "Yes. Job's complaints were reasonable." There are many in the Christian community who think this is a misguided conclusion, but I do not believe it is fair to God or Job to draw the typical conclusions. If we were in Job's place, we might have a different picture of the things that had happened. If we were wealthy but lost our fortune, if we had raised ten children who enjoyed the company of one another but had lost them all, if we were suffering every hour from sores that covered our bodies, we just might justify articulating a complaint or two. Job did. From the content of this chapter, I want us to consider three reasons why Job's complaints were reasonable.

First, Job had a limited perspective. He had no view of eternity and no knowledge of the future. There are serious limits to what we know and can know while confined to the limitations of earth. Tomorrow is a mystery. Heaven, hell, angels, and cherubim are little more than words. Thankfully, God is gracious and provides what we need. As human beings, we are limited. We are limited by space; we can be in only one place at a time. We are limited by strength; we cannot do whatever we want. We are limited by time. In distinction, God exists in eternity. There is no passing of time in eternity; God sees the past, the present, and the future as though they are an ever-present now. He is not moved by the anticipation of the future or depressed by past regrets; He lives with all of time in the present. Now is God's only time frame.

Because we live in time, it is almost impossible for us to think otherwise. We have a yesterday, we are living today, and we anticipate a tomorrow. Our thought processes work within the limits and structures of time, but this was not the verbal structure for Job. He thought in terms of actual and potential; he could not think outside of time. He, like all of us, was created in time, while God exists in eternity.

In addition to time versus eternity, it is important to consider the spiritual source of Job's challenges. He was a physical being living in the temporal world, while the conflict was spiritual and in heaven. He had no capacity to roll back the curtain of the physical to examine the spiritual. He did not know what had transpired between God and Satan. He was not there when God gave Satan permission to remove his possessions or inflict his sufferings. Job did not have a clue regarding the events in the spiritual arena. Job's perspective was limited, and so is ours. Let us not forget that on occasion God gives us insight into the spiritual realm. Praise God!

Clarity is another issue. We do not know with absolute certainty what is happening or why, and neither did Job. Limited perspective, knowledge, and understanding are reasons to complain. Uncertainty is one of humanity's biggest struggles. Nevertheless, Job was certain about who God was. Job's complaints were with his circumstances, not God.

An additional challenge with Job's perspective was the fact that he had limited revelation. There are some things we have that Job did not. One is the cross, God's intervention. We have the Scriptures, God's declaration. We have the abiding Holy Spirit, God's presence. These are real advantages. We are blessed. Job did not have any of these. He had only the traditions and history passed down from previous generations. These would have included creation, the flood, the tower of Babel, and other oral traditions. These would have been the limits of Job's revelation. To our knowledge, there were no written documents. It is amazing that God could have considered him a blameless and upright man. He was pointed out as unique; there was no one like him on earth (Job 1:8). Because of his limited perspective, complaining about his circumstances was very reasonable.

In addition to the problems of perspective, our second point is the reasonableness of verbal expression. We should expect and promote emotional communication, both sides of the emotional swing. If we are elated about the events of life, we need to express that. If we are overwhelmed by the sorrows of life, that too needs a voice. Touchdowns and home runs will generate shouts and yells of joy, while polite applause goes up for golf or tennis successes. We have an internal well of emotion that seeks expression; it is whom God has made us as communicative beings in His image. Communication is an aspect of His and our characters. Why would we think God does not want or allow our expressions on the negative side of the spectrum? When we are struggling, when we are suffering, when we are in a place we do not recognize, when we are asking why, it is not wrong to communicate disorientation, discontent, or dissatisfaction. Why would we think God would be offended when the emotions He created in us find verbal expression? He knows our thoughts and feelings. Our Bible forms this opinion, not our culture. These expressions are reasonable. When the trials, sufferings, and challenges of life well up in us and vent, it is reasonable.

Now that we have oriented our thinking to a biblical point of view, let us consider this from Job's experience. When Job lost his children, he responded in his theological understanding that God gave and God took away (Job 1:21). However, that is not a substitute for our grief. Our spirituality will not replace our social and emotional emptiness because of such a loss. Paul did not say we do not grieve; he said we do not grieve as those who have no hope (1 Thess. 4:13). Grieving is not just a silent activity; an auditory response is reasonable and often necessary.

We are creatures of communication; our expressions of pain are as reasonable as our outbursts of joy; they are both legitimate expressions of our hearts. When God invited us to come boldly or with confidence into His presence (Heb. 4:16), He did not limit us to bringing only the good things, the joyous experiences, the positive aspects of life. God wants all of us—all our experiences, thoughts and feelings. He does not want us hiding in a pretend reality or deceiving ourselves or anyone else. Job's honest expressions of grief to his friends were reasonable. He was expressing his heart openly and honestly to those who had come to comfort him.

47

Job was struggling, and rightly so. He considered God to be his friend (29:2–4). Job was expressing his heart to God as well as his friends. We can reasonably share our joys, expectations, anger and frustrations with others. God has invited us to come into His presence to minister to our hearts. If we are unwilling to bring our unsettled emotions into His presence, we limit His ministry of peace to our agitated hearts. We need to be the child who runs in from outside, the door slamming behind us, grabbing mom, and bursting into tears. We fell down and got hurt; Johnny next door took the ball; Suzy made fun of us. We are hurting, and our hearts are broken. In addition to the tears, we vent our raw, unguarded unhappiness and frustration. We want to be held and comforted. Our booboos need kisses. We need to hear, "It will be okay." We are not going to wait outside until it gets better. We are not interested in a rational discussion about the facts or the circumstances. We do not need to be told it is wrong or inappropriate to express our pain. We need to run to the presence of our rescuer to seek comfort because of the hurt. Job's expressions of pain were reasonable. He needed to be comforted.

Some may think that is not very mature. True, but it is childlike. Jesus said, "Truly I say to you, unless you are converted and become like children, you will not enter the kingdom of heaven. Whoever, then humbles himself as this child, he is the greatest in the kingdom of heaven" (Matt. 18:3–4). On another occasion, He said, "Let the children alone, and do not hinder them from coming to Me; for the kingdom of heaven belongs to such as these" (Matt. 19:14). Children tend to be honest and uninhibited in their expressions. They have not learned to be pretentious or two-faced. They are eager to learn and ready to please. Some of our concepts of maturity may have their limitations, especially in the kingdom of God. In childlike faith, Job's expressions of grief were reasonable.

Maturity may cause us to stand outside and tell ourselves that He does not want to be bothered with our pain or that He would not really understand. Maturity may cause us to tell ourselves that we do not have the words to appropriately express our frustration or that God will think less of our raw expressions of pain. Maturity may cause us to believe that He wants to hear only the good stuff and that everything is going well. We think God will have a lower opinion of us if He learns what is really happening in our lives. Get over it! God already knows. He is waiting on us to be honest in His presence. It is His desire to lavish His comfort, grace and love on us. He is willing to demonstrate His mercy in a fashion beyond our comprehension.

Job's honest expressions of hurt were reasonable because of his limited perspectives and because God solicits the expressions of our hearts. Last, they were reasonable because he never condemned God. He did not ask, "Why did You take my children? Why did You take all my cattle, sheep and camels? Why did You kill my servants?" He never blamed God for the circumstances, trials, frustrations or pains he faced. There is a world of difference between complaint and condemnation, but we are prone to blur the difference. I do not believe God has a problem with our complaints; I think He has a big problem with our condemnation. Getting Job to condemn God was Satan's goal, and it is his goal for you and me. In the first chapter, we were told of the challenge. Satan claimed that if God took Job's wealth, family, and health, he would curse God to His face (Job 1:11). We need to understand he wanted to make Job's life miserable to such an extent that he would condemn God. It did not happen. God won. That is why God could say, "Consider My servant Job, a blameless and upright man." He was God's champion.

It is important to understand the end of the story, particularly as we begin to discuss the interaction between Job and Eliphaz, Bildad and Zophar. To grasp the eternal truths of Job, we need the perspective and conclusions God provided at the end of the story, in Job 42:7–8. After Job interacted with his friends and Elihu expressed his opinions, God entered the discussion. Job and God interacted for a while. At the end of their conversation, these verses give us God's conclusion.

ROBERT W. BUTLER

> It came about after the Lord had spoken these words to Job that the Lord said to Eliphaz the Temanite, "My wrath is kindled against you and against your two friends, because you have not spoken of Me what is right as My servant Job has. Now therefore, take for yourselves seven bulls and seven rams, and go to My servant Job, and offer up a burnt offering for yourselves, and My servant Job will pray for you. For I will accept him so that I may not do with you according to your folly, because you have not spoken of Me what is right, as My servant Job has."

He repeated Himself so we would not miss the point. Job had spoken what was right; Eliphaz and his friends had not. That is an important truth to maintain as we move through the rest of the concepts in this book. As we look at issues that may push our comfort zones, we must keep straight who is right and who is wrong. This chapter is a good start. As we read Job's complaints, we may think we do not want to hear this. The more important question is whether God wants us to hear it. Were Job's complaints reasonable? The short answer is yes, because his perspectives were limited. Yes, because God is a God who invites the expression of the heart. Yes, because he did not condemn God for his circumstances.

In our own struggles with the difficulties of life, we may need Job's paraphrase of Paul, "Complain, and yet do not sin" (Eph. 4:26). Your perspectives are limited. Your invitation into the presence of God is a standing offer. Do not blame God for the trials and difficulties. Take your complaint into the presence of God, solicit His comfort, and find grace in His presence.

50

CHAPTER 6

God, the Judge

Job 4:1–7:21

This chapter, which takes us into the middle section of Job, begins the three cycles of speeches between Job and his friends. Eliphaz begins in each cycle; his first speech is in chapters 4 and 5. Job responds in chapters 6 and 7. As you read chapters 4 and 5, you may find yourself in agreement with Eliphaz, thinking his expressions sound like ideas from Psalms or Proverbs. Perhaps it will feel similar to Romans or in line with James. Our minds may run through this catalog of Scriptures that will seemingly support the arguments and contentions of Eliphaz in his challenge of Job.

In this chapter, however, we are not going down that road. Right up front we need to remind ourselves that we know the end of the book. God is victorious. While Satan is going to marshal his forces with cunning, God is still going to win. The battle is over Job's service and submission to God. Satan said it was about the things God had done for Job, and God contended it was about the relationship He had with Job. The truth of this is found when we come to the end of the book (Job 42), when God interacted with Job and Eliphaz. Though it seems reasonable to assume all of the participants were there, God told Eliphaz he needed to make sacrifice and have Job pray for him because he had not spoken what was right about Him as had His servant, Job (42:7).

So as we study and read Job, we must remember that Eliphaz, Bildad, and Zophar did not speak what was right about God; Job did. In our own struggles and difficult circumstances, we need to remind ourselves that at the end of story, God won. It is also important to remember that there is a spiritual plane we do not see or understand. It is our relationship with God that matters.

Rather than comparing Eliphaz's words with the rest of Scripture, we need to look at his words in the broader context of his ideas and assertions about God. We need the bigger context of what he said to accurately understand his statements. We need to remember that this was about God, not Job. We need to be careful not to get lost in the suffering of Job or the contentions of his friends regarding his behavior. Job's friends were drawing conclusions about who God was and His expectations in the world. As we consider the exchanges between Job and his friends in this and the next twenty-six chapters of Job, we will need this perspective to stay on track with God's conclusions.

At the time Job lived, there was no written revelation. There were no chosen people. This story precedes or is concurrent with Abraham, Isaac, and Jacob. God is sharing His heart and who He is with the world. God has always made Himself known in the world (Rom. 1:19–20). These exchanges clarify the difference between what humanity, particularly religious humanity, tends to think, and what God wants us to know.

After reading chapter 5, the complaint meter in heaven may have gone up significantly. I believe God was thinking it was good that His people were sharing their hearts with Him. As you recall, we asked, "Was Job's complaining reasonable?" The simple answer was yes, it was absolutely reasonable. We drew that conclusion for three reasons. The first was because our perspectives may be limited. Job knew he was in a bad place and did not like it. Second, complaining was reasonable because God invites us into His presence to express our hearts to Him. God invited all of me, all of my life, all of my experiences to commune with Him. God knows everything. I may not be happy about a long list of situations, circumstances, and relationships not going well, but God wants to hear about it. Jesus wants to live His life in me (Gal. 2:20). Third, it was reasonable as long as we did not condemn or blame God for the circumstances of life. It is reasonable as long as we honor God.

After Job expressed his complaints in the last chapter, Eliphaz, Bildad, and Zophar must have thought they had the grounds to communicate with Job. It is reasonable to assume that either separately or together they pondered and maybe discussed the causes of Job's suffering and loss. As we look at these speeches, monologues, arguments, and condemnations by his friends, we are going to see the conclusions they drew about Job's circumstances that were built on their assumptions and opinions about God, who He is and how He operates in the world. So as we begin our examination of Eliphaz's speech, let us ask, "What kind of judge is God?" Our answer to that question will significantly impact the way we live.

Have you ever known people who lived as though they felt guilty all the time? I have known those who said they did not feel they had been to church if they did not feel guilty. They live as though God is sitting at His judicial bench in heaven, wrapped in His legal robe with His gavel poised, ready, waiting, and anticipating the opportunity to say, "Guilty!" In their minds they are doing it for Him. Too many people live with a view of God as an exacting judge sitting on His throne pronouncing judgment. That is a really bad view of God. While God is going to pronounce judgment, He is not awaiting the opportunity to come down on us. This is the major problem Eliphaz has with God.

Let us consider the text. This is an Eastern document, and there were formal patterns to their exchanges. The first several verses of chapter 4 are the culturally appropriate polite introduction to the conversation in Eliphaz's preparation to confront Job. From verses 7 through 11, we can make our first observation about Eliphaz's perception of God. (Read these verses.) If we take his comments as a complete thought, Eliphaz saw God as a black-and-white, cause-and-effect judge. You do well, you get good things; you do badly, you get bad things. God was just waiting for you to act and would respond with one or the other. People were in control of God; their behavior controlled what God did. If you were upright and righteous, you would be blessed; if you caused problems, there would be no end to your grief. You and your actions and your attitudes were in control of what God was going to do; you controlled your destiny and were the master of your fate. In Eliphaz's mind, God was merely an adjudicator of your behavior who punished or rewarded in direct response to your actions, thoughts, attitudes, character, and so on.

Eliphaz's analysis was wrong. It was unbiblical. His conclusions were contrary to the concept of God's grace, the reason Jesus came to die for us while we were still sinners (Rom. 5:8). Eden was a perfect environment. Humanity in Adam chose to rebel against the directions of God (Rom. 5:12). In spite of man's choices and poor behavior, God was willing to pursue a relationship with mankind. We did not deserve God's investment. God made a gracious choice.

Contrary to Eliphaz's conclusions, God is a gracious judge. God is not this black-and-white, you had your chance, intolerant arbiter. Humanity, especially religious humanity, approaches life from this perspective, but God does not. What goes around does not come around because God is a God of grace.

Eliphaz told Job he had had his chance, had done what was wrong, and his suffering was the evidence, the result of what he did or did not do. He needed to repent for his errant behavior so God could bless him. Because Job had sinned, he was suffering. If he repented, God would bless him. While that was the argument Eliphaz made, it did not represent who God is. Certainly there is a truth that and individual will reap what he or she sows (Gal. 6:7–8). However, that is about humanity and the nature of the world in which we live, not God.

Second, contrary to Eliphaz's assumption, God is a gracious judge because He can be satisfied. Eliphaz claimed because God cannot be satisfied, of necessity Job had failed God and was experiencing the consequences of his poor behavior. In verses 17 and 18, Eliphaz stated his view that it was impossible to please God, that not even the angels were capable of measuring up to God's expectations. By logical necessity, there was no way mankind could be approved before God. Since the angels did not, clearly Job could not. The proof was in the reality of his suffering. Therefore, he needed to repent for the error of his ways. However, that misrepresented God. God can be satisfied. His justice can be met. God is reasonable. Even though God has a standard of perfection (Matt. 5:48) and has not changed, He has made it possible for the standard to be met—in Jesus.

Jesus stands before the Father and says, "I paid it all" (1 John 2:1–2). The penalty of sin has been paid. Here is my blood taken to the Holy of Holies (Heb. 9:11–12). Sin has been forgiven. The forgiven measure up; they are perfect. We know our own weaknesses; we know our own failures; we know our propensity to blame God even if we are not suffering like Job. That is who we are. But God has His justice satisfied in Jesus by grace. Yet Eliphaz left no ground for man's failures to be satisfied before God. He had no plan for God not to punish. There was no place where one could find forgiveness or freedom in the presence of God. Repentance may come after judgment, but God was obligated to judge. Let us read Job 4:17: "Can man be just before God? Can a man be pure before his Maker?" The answer that Job knew was yes, but Eliphaz assumed no. "He put no trust even in His servants and against His angels He charges error." God is black and white; He waits for the opportunity to inflict justice. "Inflict" seems to capture Eliphaz's perception. There will be a time for justice. However, the verb "inflict" does not give us an appropriate understanding of God. He is a gracious, merciful judge who can be satisfied.

The third errant assumption about God in Eliphaz's speech is in chapter 5, verse 8 through the balance of the chapter. In the first seven verses, Eliphaz gave examples to support his argument, trying to establish that Job was not an exception to the rule but rather an illustration of it. God was a black-and-white judge who operated strictly in a cause-and-effect relationship, and the results were immediate. If you did poorly, you paid the price; if you did well, you were blessed. Eliphaz did not view God as a patient judge. He was an exacting, intolerant, almost sinister judge. Sin had to be dealt with immediately. There was urgency to God's judicial actions. There were no second chances, no waiting until tomorrow. According to Eliphaz's understanding and argument, God had no patience.

According to Eliphaz, it was obvious Job has suffered for a considerable amount of time. Therefore, not only had Job sinned, he had also not repented. If he had only repented, the problems would have stopped. The continuance of the suffering was indicative of a lack of repentance as well as the severity of his sin. Eliphaz believed there was a direct and immediate relationship between Job's failures, his lack of repentance, and the ongoing nature of his troubles. If we have the same view of God, we will make the same determinations. We will have the same frustration and the same dissatisfaction with God.

Job responded in chapters 6 and 7. In contrast to Eliphaz's view, Job's speech contended that God was gracious, just, and patient. Job said, "Nonsense. God is in control." Job argued the complete antithesis regarding God's response to man's actions. Job had placed his total trust in the God he worshiped and knew. He made sacrifice; he entered into the presence of God. He would do what God had asked humanity to do. He had absolute faith in the fact that God was still God and in control of heaven and earth. God was the decision maker. God was in control for His own purposes (Prov. 16:4).

Job made an interesting observation. "For the despairing man there should be kindness from his friend; so that he does not forsake the fear of the Almighty" (Job 6:14). This was to counter what Eliphaz had done to Job. If God was in control for His own purposes, which was why He should be feared and the cause of suffering, friends should show kindness. They should not be an additional burden to bear. If friends are not supportive in times of struggle, they may be friends like Job's. It may be time for new friends. We all need friends who will support our faithfulness and not drive us from God. Job declared that Eliphaz had a wrong view of God, that he was misrepresenting God and was not being a supportive friend. Because he lacked an accurate view of God, he could not understand what was happening. Job told Eliphaz that true friends were supportive both of the relationship and the commitment to serving God.

This is an important aspect of our interaction with those we know, those we spend time with, and those who are involved in our lives. We all will have challenges in our lives. Too often Satan is doing the same thing he did with Job, trying to get us to deny or condemn the God of heaven and His grace, patience and mercy. God is a merciful God, and Job was committed to a relationship with Him. Job contended that his friends should have supported his commitment to Almighty God.

In Job 6:24, we find the second response by Job. He demanded the specifics of Eliphaz's generic accusations. He asked, "If I erred, what did I do?" Point it out. Declare the exact mistakes. What is it I did or did not do? What are the problems with my attitude? If you are going to be helpful by suggesting I repent, of what do I repent? Your ill-reasoned arguments prove nothing.

The verses starting at the beginning of chapter 7 build Job's argument that freedom is in God. Hopefully, you have experienced the freedom from sin. I trust that you have experienced biblical freedom from guilt. I desire that you are experiencing the freedom from frustration because God is in control. You are living in God's peace if you are growing and developing your understanding of the freedom you have in Jesus Christ. Job was living in the freedom he had in his relationship with the God of heaven who was in control.

Some have trouble with Job wanting freedom from the excruciating pain he was experiencing. He told God he would choose death rather than pain (7:15). The short route to freedom from the circumstances of his life and the agony of his body was to die (7:21). He understood God was in control of everything, including life and death. This expression was part of his answer to Eliphaz's errant view of God being controlled by men. God was just, gracious, patient, and in control for His own purposes. Job's right view of God will change our view of the world.

In Psalm 73:2–9, we find the psalmist struggling with his view of the world. It appeared that the wicked were prospering from their behavioral rejection of God's standards and expectations. The psalmist at this point was dealing with the opposite view of Eliphaz, who had claimed the wicked were judged right here, immediately. It was the righteous who were blessed. However, that was not the observation of the psalmist. He told us based on observation that the wicked were getting away with their ungodly actions and attitudes and not being judged. He seemed to feel the world was out of order, the bad guys were winning, and the good guys were losing. Job did not stand alone in his claim that Eliphaz did not represent a godly worldview. The truth of the psalmist's frustration is a repudiation of Eliphaz's line of reasoning about God. In verses 15 and following, the psalmist recognized the error of such a claim. As he understood a broader spiritual perspective, he learned God was patient in His judgment. At some time, the wicked will receive the just consequences of their actions. Judgment is not immediate.

The psalmist shared Job's view that God was in control. "You set them." "You cast them down." It was also in His timing, "when aroused." It is when God was ready to deal with the situation that He acted for His purposes. When God's patience ran out, it was time for the scales of justice to be balanced. When grace came to an end, then the wicked received the appropriate consequences for their actions and attitudes, but it would be in God's determined time.

Personally, I am with Eliphaz. I want the wicked to be punished right now, but in God's court of justice, it does not work that way. Fortunately, the psalmist helped us to understand Job's argument. The end of Psalm 73 says:

> 25 Whom have I in heaven but You?
> And besides You, I desire nothing on earth.
> 26 My flesh and my heart may fail,
> But God is the strength of my heart and my portion forever.
> 28 But as for me, the nearness of God is my good;
> I have made the Lord GOD my refuge,
> That I may tell of all Your works.

Can you hear Job expressing these words back to Eliphaz? He was saying that the Lord was his refuge. He had made Him his support and strength. God would deal with the bad guys when He got around to it.

We need to see God as gracious, just, and patient. It is in His time, not ours. We must allow God to be God. Your friends should be helping you with this perspective, and so should your church.

CHAPTER 7
God Is Just
Job 8:1–10:22

I trust you have discovered that Job is a fascinating book and that it is not about suffering or grief of life or about thoughtless or difficult friends. It deals with the character of God. Those other issues are a part of the story, but they are not the point or theme of Job. God wanted to roll back the uncertainty of time and give us insight into His character and nature and the operation of eternity. It was His intent to provide us with comfort, encouragement, and understanding particularly in the face of the unexplainable. Job is about the one we love, serve, and worship, who still seeks worshipers (John 4:23). The scenes in heaven and the exchanges with his friends tell us about who God is and is not.

In the last chapter, we looked at Eliphaz's first speech, and in this chapter it is Bildad's turn. Job's friends have lots of points to make. There are three cycles of speeches or exchanges, though Zophar will skip his turn in the last cycle. Each of the eight speeches addresses a different aspect of God's character. In this chapter we explore Bildad's concern for God's justice. It is important to remind ourselves that at the beginning of the book, God said, "Consider my servant Job; there is none like him" (Job 1:8). At the end of the book, He told Eliphaz,

"You have not spoken well of me like my servant Job has" (Job 42:7). So God reaffirmed that Job's words represent who God was and were legitimate expressions for our understanding of God's grace and mercy as well as his investment in the lives of people. On the flip side, Eliphaz, Bildad, and Zophar had not grasped the God of eternity, the God of the Bible.

When we read these speeches, we could easily get trapped by the logic of Job's friends if we did not remind ourselves of God's conclusions. Their arguments make perfect sense from our human religious perspective, but they are wrong. We all have known people who were logical but wrong; we need reminders to maintain our equilibrium and clarity on God's perspective.

Turn to the book of Job, chapter 8. As we looked at Eliphaz's speech in the last chapter, we asked ourselves what kind of judge God was. In the exchange between Eliphaz and Job, we saw God was gracious, just, and patient. Eliphaz's contentions were built on ideas that these things were not true about God. Eliphaz appealed to the wisdom handed down from previous generations. His understanding of God was not one of personal relationship.

Bildad picked up on an issue Eliphaz had raised. I want us to consider the question, "How do we understand God's justice?" This was the focus of Bildad's speech and Job's response. Let me encourage you to read the first five verses. These will set the context for us. Bildad claimed that people got what they had coming. He told Job that his children had been sinners and had died; get over it. His logic was that this should be obvious because they were dead. Bildad lacked compassion in his assertion; he was assuming God's judgment was in the present, and in this sense he shared Eliphaz's perspective. We find in some segments of the church a similar view of God. If God is going to bless you, He is going to bless you here and now. If He is going to judge you, He is going to judge you here and now. You are going to experience the consequences of your behavior in the present. Bildad's argument was that Job's children had sinned and had died. He believed God implemented His decisions only in the here and now. In the temporal realm, He blessed or judged based on people's behaviors, values, and character.

Have you heard anything like that? If you spend much time listening to preachers, you certainly will hear similar ideas. We need to be discerning how people use the Word of God from Genesis to Revelation. We must follow the full counsel of God, particularly in our understanding of the God of the Bible.

In answering, "How do we understand God's justice?" Bildad provided us the first insight on the negative side. God's justice is not necessarily in the here and now; it may be in eternity. We look at this issue in Psalm 73, in which the psalmist said he was watching the prosperity of the wicked and asked, "What gives here?" The question was raised because he was looking only at the present; he had this issue with God until he came into the house of the Lord. In His presence, from His perspective, he perceived their end. There is justice in eternity, not necessarily in time.

When Jesus healed the blind man, this same logic surfaced (John 9). The disciples asked, "Who sinned? Did this man sin or his parents?" They were still thinking that sin had consequences right here, right now. If you have a problem in your life, it is because you have sinned; at least somebody must have sinned. But justice is not necessarily in time. According to Jesus, the blindness was not due to the blind man's or his parents' sins; it was for the glory of God (John 9:3). It is important we understand who God is, not who we want Him to be. In God's grace, in God's eternal counsel, in God's understanding of the past, the present, and the future, justice is certain. God knows who we are and where He is taking us. Our current bad experiences may not be anything we want to brag about: "I got to suffer! I was so excited about it!"

Daniel's friends, Shadrach, Meshach, and Abed-nego, had to face the challenge of Nebuchadnezzar's idol to which they were supposed to bow down (Dan. 3). Their response was that their God could deliver them from the furnace, but they wanted it known that whether He did or did not, they were not going to bow down. I am sure that as the guard was preparing them to be tossed into the fiery furnace, the three friends were not saying, "Well, this is a day we're going to remember." I think they were making peace with God, getting ready to meet their maker. All the experiences of life do not directly correlate, as Bildad wanted us to think. Have you ever done what is right and suffered for it? I am sure everyone has heard the often-true phrase, "No good deed goes unpunished."

Bildad did not understand who our God is. God has a much bigger picture of life and reality. He sees our lives, past, present, and future. Justice may have to wait for another day. I hate that, and I am sure you do too! I want to see "them" pay the price. I could have been one of Job's friends. Sadly, Christian writers and speakers conclude that Job got what he had deserved in spite of God's declarations. It seems to be the way we are religiously wired.

The second truth about God's justice in this exchange is in Job 9. In response to Bildad, Job expanded upon the fact that mankind is guilty before God. God's justice demands a verdict of guilty. It will help to read chapter 9 as we discuss man's guilt. In summary of chapter 9, Job said in paraphrase, "Bildad, what's your point? Mankind is guilty before God; it is who we are. That's our problem. So why are you carrying on?" Job understood that humanity was guilty before God. Job moved from the generic statement into some specific expressions of frustration over the next several verses. In verse 13 he said, "God will not turn back His anger." In the next verse he declared, "How then can I answer Him, and choose my words before Him?" Let us jump down to verse 28. "I know that you will not acquit me." He continued in verses 30 and 31, "If I should wash myself with snow and cleanse my hands with lye, yet you would plunge me into the pit, my own clothes would abhor me."

Earlier in the context, he talked about being made by God. We know from Psalm 139 that we were woven together; the parts of our being were written in God's book. We have in

Jeremiah that wonderful picture of the potter and clay (Jer. 18). God speaks of shaping and fashioning on the wheel as it spins. If you have ever watched a potter with fascination, you have seen the immediacy of his creativity and absolute control. The potter is a wonderful visual of God's investment in our lives. The potter shapes and fashions each piece of clay as he chooses. Isaiah equates this creative endeavor with our lives. God shapes and fashions us; He knows us. Job was saying, "I know I am guilty. I know I stand condemned before You. Cut me some slack!" This was the expression of Job's heart.

If we are going to understand God's justice, we must understand we are guilty before God; that is the reality of our humanity Romans 3 makes clear. There is none righteous, not one. Their feet are swift to shed blood. The poison of asps is under their lips. The passage concludes in verse 23 with the blanket condemnation that everyone has sinned. In Romans 6, Paul gives us the results of our sin: "The wages of sin is death." We are guilty before God. If we are going to understand God's justice, mercy, and love, we have to understand we are in desperate need of it. We fail to understand God's awesome goodness because we think we are good enough to have earned it, deserved it, or justified it. But we do not! We cannot. We have lost sight of the fact that in our flesh, in our humanity, we are separated from the holy, righteous God of eternity. God's justice will rightly condemn us. This fact needs to be an emotional, functional reality in our lives. If it is only an academic, intellectual exercise with which we agree, we do not understand God's justice.

I was involved in Christian education for many years. In 1998, the Association of Christian Schools International published *Reclaiming the Future of Christian Education*, which addressed the issue of why Christian education had not lived up to its promise. It was supposed to produce committed Christian young men and women who were going to change the world. You may have noticed over the last forty years not a whole lot of that has happened, and the book was written in part to answer why not. I am not going to give you the answer from the book; I am going to give you my answer to that question. My answer resides in exactly what we are addressing with God's justice. It was my observation that many young Christians, whether in Christian schools or churches, have held the concept of their sinfulness only as a theological idea. They would agree we are all sinners, but unfortunately they have not brought that concept into the reality of who they are. They have not applied it to "I" am a sinner; "I" stand separated from God; "I" am guilty. Sinners are what "other" people are.

I remember when God worked me over on that issue. I was one of those young Christians who could have made no significant impact on the world because of my arrogance. I believed God and I could change the world, but the problem was that God did not need my help, and I sadly did not understand that. God had to reveal to me that in my flesh and apart from his grace and mercy, I was capable of the most heinous of any crimes imaginable or unimaginable. That is who I was; that is who I am. Until I could wrap my mind around my condition before God, I was arrogant, caustic, angry, and even hateful because I did not emotionally or spiritually accept I was a sinner. Once God enabled me to understand I was a sinner separated from Him, having grown up in church did not make much of a dent in my behavior. It had to be His Spirit at work in my life transforming me. Then God could deal with the anger, hate, bitterness, and caustic behavior. Then God's grace could come alive because suddenly I realized I was a sinner and I stood condemned before God. This was not theory but what was rightly true about me. I understood I was in desperate need of His mercy and grace and saving kindness in my life. As I understood my spiritual condition, God could transform me. I could become a different person. My character and values could change. I recognized God spent a lot of time shaping and fashioning the person I have become; it is not the person in my flesh. That is the importance of understanding that we stand guilty before God. Until we can wrap our minds around this truth, we really do not understand from what we have been saved. As long as I think I can change myself, I live in my religious arrogance. I reject or refuse to embrace the biblical truth that nothing good inhabits my flesh (Rom. 7:18). The flesh and the Spirit of God are enemies (Gal. 5:17).

Job had awesome insight into the character of God. These next few verses are amazing. He recognized he stood condemned. At Job 9:32 he said,

> For He is not a man as I am that I may answer Him, that we may go to court together. There is no umpire [there is no referee; there is no one who can mediate] between us, who may lay his hand upon us both. Let Him remove his rod from me, and let not dread of Him terrify me. Then I would speak and not fear Him, but I am not like that in myself.

This is a picture of what Jesus has done for us. When I understand as Job did that I am separated from God, then I recognize I have a desperate need and have no place to go to appeal God's decision. I accept I cannot stand in His presence. I have no doubt I need someone who can mediate.

Job used a word picture to describe how issues were settled in his day. A wise individual of equal status to both parties would lay his hands on both as they presented their cases and then render a verdict. Today, in the spiritual realm, Jesus does this. He is fully God, fully man, standing between us (Phil. 2:6–8). In 1 John 2:1 we learn that Jesus is our Mediator who stands between a just God and our sinfulness. Jesus, between God and humanity, hung on a cross in our place. He is the one who can place his hand on God and mankind and invite us into the presence of God. Job understood what needed to be done. Because of his relationship with God, he shared the insight of his heart's need. He needed someone to mediate with God. Praise God! Because of His justice, we have a mediator, which God's justice requires.

Job shared this truth from his relationship with God and explained to Bildad that he had it all wrong. Justice may not be in the here and now. Yes, we are guilty before God. We need someone who can stand in the presence of God and plead our case. Job understood he did not have standing before God. What an awesome picture. God's justice will happen in His time. In God's justice, we are guilty and thus separated from Him. But He has provided Jesus as a mediator who can plead our cases. That is the good news of the gospel we have to share with a world still separated from a loving God.

There is one more aspect of God's justice Job wanted to address. God's justice is as certain as the sunrise, as sure as death and taxes. In the first verse of chapter 10, Job was struggling with his condition. "I loathe my own life; I will give full vent to my complaint." He was struggling to understanding what was happening. In verse 7 he said, "According to your knowledge I am indeed not guilty, yet there is no deliverance from Your hand." While judgment was certain, it did not provide an explanation for his experience. He knew he had done what God required of him. He knew he was guilty but nevertheless had done what God had expected. He was struggling with his experiences. Interestingly, he accepted his lack of understanding because he knew judgment was certain. In verse 8, he talked about the fact he was made by God's hand and questioned if He would destroy him. He acknowledged all the ways in which God actively invested in creating him and preserving his life. Still, he was expressing his bewilderment at trying to grasp what was happening. Because he asserted he was a unique creation of God and God had fashioned him, he expressed his knowledge that God had a right to judge and that judgment was certain. In support of God's certain justice, Job stated in verse 14, "If I sin, then you would take note of me, and would not acquit me of my guilt." The next couple of verses are a continued affirmation of certain justice. If I am guilty, sin will be punished; that is the certainty of God's justice.

Justice may not be in the here and now. We, in our flesh, are guilty before God, whose justice is certain. Praise God! We have a mediator. So what does that mean to you and me? How do we apply these truths today? Job expressed the question this way in Job 10:18: "Why then have you brought me out of the womb?" We may experience Job's frustrations and complaints. It is possible you are there now. The truth from Job is that we may not understand our present circumstance. Job had no grasp of what was going on in his life. He experienced the loss of his children, wealth, health, and through these dialogues the loss of his friends. Like Job, we may not understand the where and why of our circumstances, but we need to cling to the certainty of God's justice as Job did. That is the decision of a champion. While it may not be in this lifetime, justice will happen. God, who is in control, understands.

The second application of God's justice is in Job 10:12. You might think in the midst of Job's complaints and Job's frustration that there would be no hope, but here is another window into his soul. This verse should catch our attention. This was Job's heart: "You have granted me life and lovingkindness; and Your care has preserved my spirit." In spite of his lack of understanding, his lack of wealth, his lack of family, the excruciating experiences with life and friends, what is the cry of his heart? You have given me life. You have given me lovingkindness. Your care preserves my spirit. In the midst of all his complaining, Job had not rejected God. Job did not condemn God for what he has experienced. Job, in spite of all his circumstances, was living out what God said to Satan in Job 1:8: "Have you considered my servant Job? There is none like him." I do not know that I would be so gracious and understanding. I do not know I could say to God, "You have granted me life and lovingkindness." I think it would be more like, "What are you thinking, God? This is awful!"

As we try to understand God's justice, let us acknowledge that we may have no ability to grasp what is happening. However, we can be certain God will be just. We can be certain there is a mediator. We can be certain His justice will be in His time, not ours. We may have to wait until eternity, but it is certain. We can be certain God is our provider and our protector. Even in experiences like Job's, we can count on his lovingkindness. God is awesome! That is the God we gather to worship.

CHAPTER 8

Real Hope

Job 11:1–14:22

We looked at the events in heaven that got Job into this mess in the first chapter. God asked Satan, "Have you considered my servant Job? There is none like him on earth" (Job 1:8). I do not know about you, but I do not think I would have been as resolute as Job. I am glad God knows how much I can handle (1 Cor. 10:13). In chapter 4, we discussed his friends coming to provide comfort. We read about their sitting in silence for seven days; they took comforting Job seriously. In the last two chapters, they began to take turns speaking, drawing on the wisdom of their day. It is a lesson about the contemporary wisdom of our day. In the first two speeches, we saw the importance of grounding our faith, hope, and expectations in the declarations of God's Word. We can find God revealed there.

In the last chapter, Bildad spoke. We asked, "How do we understand God's justice?" Bildad thought it was in the here and now; Job disagreed. Just as the psalmist loosely declared in Psalm 73, "I saw the wicked prosper, and it bugged me." Second, they agreed for different reasons that humanity is guilty and rightly deserved condemnation. Mankind does not stand blameless before God; humanity has a problem.

Justice requires that the guilt be resolved. Job understood that if he was going to experience justice, he needed a mediator. Job asked, "Where is the man who can put his hand on God and his hand on man?" (Job 9:33). It was a wonderful picture of Jesus standing between God and man. The last point of contention between Bildad and Job was differing perspectives about the certainty of justice. God, as a just God, would bring about justice in His time for His purposes.

Before we consider Zophar's first speech, let us remind ourselves of God's perspective. God declared Job to be a righteous man who was pleasing to Him (Job 1:8). He raised the issue with Satan at the beginning and told Eliphaz at the end of the story that Job had spoken what was right about God and they had not (Job 42:7). In reading the book of Job, especially these speeches, it is easy to lose track of who is right and who is wrong. Fortunately, God declared Job's friends were wrong in their representations of who He was. Even if we do not have a problem with the assertions of Job's friends, God did. Because this is a book about God, it is important to understand accurately who spoke right and who spoke wrong. The speeches between Job and his friends are particularly helpful to clarify God's character, motivation, and actions.

It would be good to read chapters 11 through 14 of Job before we consider Zophar's first speech. Zophar spoke in chapter 11, and Job took the next three chapters to respond. The word "hope" appears several times in these four chapters, so we are going to ask, "What is the basis of our hope? Why can we have hope? What is the source of our hope?" Because hopelessness is man's natural condition, we need hope! We do not want to live in despair, the worst place to be. In difficult times, at life's worst junctures, we often lose hope. We feel as though we will never escape the messes consuming our thoughts and energies. But when hope takes root in our hearts, it is like the lifting of a dark cloud. It begins to feel as though a weight has been lifted off our chests. A light appears, and there seems to be the possibility there is an end to our dark tunnel. Even though we are still struggling, things seem a little better. They may not be any better, but hope anticipates a better tomorrow. When we have hope, we can see or at least believe that God is moving and that something is changing. Hope is an important aspect of our spirituality as well as our humanity. Without hope, we live in the quagmire of despair. In these chapters, Zophar is going to offer some suggestions about hope that are contrary to God's perspective. Job follows with his observations. Their comments will lead us in the direction of both appropriate and inappropriate sources of hope. It is important to understand what leads us to success or failure.

Zophar's prescription for Job's restoration to blessing is in Job 11:13–19. Zophar's solution was simple; Job just needed to repent of the evil he was harboring (11:14). If he would only choose to do what was right, everything would be wonderful. We like the sound and the simplicity of that. Unfortunately, it is so appealing that this same concept can be found in overt and subtle forms among Christians. While the words change, the idea is the same. If we are willing to work hard at getting our act together, God will bless us, and we will get an A for effort.

However, it was not true then, and it is not true now. This concept is founded in paganism, not biblical Christianity. It appeals to our religious need to appease the gods to garner their favors and blessings. That does not represent the God of the Bible or His operation in the world. While we were sinners, Jesus died for us (Rom. 5:8). Grace is the unmerited favor of God. We cannot merit it before or after salvation.

Zophar missed the point. Let me explain why this lacked biblical substance and was not a good idea. Hope does not reside in our repentance. Repentance is a significant theological idea. I trust that God, through His Spirit, has moved you to repent. Nevertheless, your hope does not rest on your repentance but on the graciousness of God according to His Word. Legally, if I repent of my crimes, I may still have to pay the price for my behavior. My repentance does not necessarily change the consequences of my actions. In our Christian circles, we think somehow repentance is the end-all, be-all, and cure-all. Absolutely not! We see too many Christians repent and engage in the same self-willed, thoughtless behavior again. Their repentance did not change them or anything else. The reason for their lack of change is usually found in the fact they really liked doing it. (Of course, this does not address addictive behaviors that can trap people in cycles of failure.) They did not have a change of mind regarding their actions; that is what repentance means. It is a change of mind, a change of heart, a change of destination, and only God can produce that kind of change.

The picture in the biblical language is that you turn around and go the other direction. When we are driving, lost, and going the wrong direction, we need to repent, to go the other way. Repentance is a realization of where we are and a commitment to change, to take a different direction. This is a process that may take some time, so it cannot be the foundation of our hope. It is also true that we can go different directions and still be going the wrong way. We can go different directions and still be unwilling to face the issues with God. Many of us have the ability and the will of character to change and do not understand why some people struggle, why they don't just decide to change. However, like Adam and Eve, people tend to find temptation irresistible.

Repentance is not a magic wand that produces the desired results. Let us consider Esau. He sold his birthright for a meal, but repentance could not get him blessed (Heb. 11:17). Repentance is not the basis of our hope. While repentance is a part of the process that leads to eternal life (Acts 11:18), it is not the source of hope. It is the kindness of God that leads us to repentance (Rom. 2:4). To put our hope in repentance is to put our hope in religious behavior, whether it is repentance, walking the aisle, raising our hands, attending the right church, or something else. While these have wonderful, even significant, meaning, they cannot be the basis of our hope. None of them will save us. The sign in front of the church is not going to get us into heaven. Yes, we should repent, attend church, and take many proper actions; I am not condemning any of these. My point is, and Job's point was, that our actions are not the basis of our hope; it is our relationship with the Creator.

My hope has to be in God. When our behavior becomes the basis of our hope, we miss biblical Christianity. We have been sucked into some kind of "religious" organization, though it could be a civic group or secret society. When we rely on the ritual or our behavior, we are separated from real hope because hope is anchored in the finished work of the cross. It is not in the rituals inside or outside church or in our actions. That is how we know Zophar was mistaken in his direction. He told Job if he did the right thing, if he repented, God would bless him. Job said he had repented, but it was obvious he was not being blessed. Job knew that Zophar was incorrect in his explanations and solutions. What God said about Job resolved any doubt. I am not condemning or challenging the importance of repentance. Nevertheless, our hope cannot be in our repentance; it cannot be the source of our hope.

The next verse in chapter 11 gives us the second element that is not the basis of our hope. "For the eyes of the wicked will fail and there will be no escape for them and there hope is to breathe their last." Zophar was seriously mistaken a second time. For the wicked, life is as good as it is going to get. When they breathe their last, there is no hope. Zophar thought that when the wicked die, their existence ends, so it has to be better for them. Zophar did not share God's perspective. Hope, particularly for the wicked, is to live, not die. Our desire as Christians should be that they never die until they are born again (John 3:3). We should pray the Spirit of God will eventually grab their hearts and draw them into relationship with Jesus. They need to understand the importance of the cross and their need of the Savior. Once they die, the decision is settled. "It is appointed for man to die once, and after this comes judgment" (Acts 9:27). There is no support anywhere in Scripture that you get a second chance. There are no do-overs. We have to address and resolve our relationship with God while we have breath. When the wicked die, they face eternal judgment. We should weep for the wicked when they die because they have moved to the ultimate state of hopelessness, an eternity separated from God. Zophar had it wrong; there is no hope in the death of the wicked, as Zophar contended.

So Job expressed it in his own way. "Zophar, you missed it. Be quiet! Just let me talk" (Job 12:2). Job talked about hope in the next three chapters; he understood the true nature of hope. He spent chapter 12 giving examples. He told Zophar he had made his point but asked if he had considered a variety of issues that did not support the nonsense he claimed. Let us consider Job 13:15. Remember Job's circumstances; he had lost his children, wealth, and health, but he declared, "Though he slay me, I will hope in him." Job's hope was firmly placed in God and his relationship with Him. His hope had not been diminished by his circumstances or increased by what he had done or could do. It was in God Himself. This verse needs to be connected to Job 14:14, "If a man dies, will he live again." Job was confident in an eternal relationship with God, and that is where our hope has to be anchored. Our hope cannot be in what we have done, what we will or will not do, what we can do, or anything else related to our behavior. Our hope has to be firmly rooted in who God is. Biblically, hope is about what God has done and will do.

When our hope is in God, it puts all life in proper perspective; we are not drawn into the foolishness of what is going on around us or the arrogance of what we can accomplish. Our hope should not be in the changing circumstances of life. We can be at peace with the fact that people are sinners and they are going to do stupid stuff; we do not have to be bothered by that. They are just living in their fallen conditions, doing what God expects them to do, being foolish, selfish, self-centered, arrogant, condescending, angry, and so on. That is who they are. That is who we are! Until the grace of God invades our hearts and begins to transform us, that was exactly what we were doing. Our hope has to be in God and His finished work. Otherwise, our lives shrivel due to our frustrations because we are allowing people and circumstances to be in control rather than God. Our hope must be in God's process (Phil. 1:6). When our hope is grounded in Him, life looks better. It is not circumstance; it is not people; it is not things that are controlling our perspectives. We are allowing God to be the potter (Rom. 9:21), the foundation of our hope.

Let's skip down a couple more verses in chapter 13. After he declared, "Though He slay me, I will hope in Him," Job expanded on his relationship with God in verse 20. "Only two things do not do to me, then I will not hide from Your face: do not remove your hand from me and let not the dreaded You terrify me." When we think about the circumstances of Job's life, we might think he would have drawn the conclusion that God had taken His hand off him and had allowed all the chaos and tragedy he had experienced. Pain and agony were still destroying his body; they were his daily reality. He had lost everything, and his wife had encouraged him to curse God and die. Nevertheless, he contended that God's hand was still on him. That is amazing! He could live beyond the circumstances because his hope was grounded in the God he knew, not on what he had had or what he had done. It was not in his friends or in wealth or poverty. He believed God's hand was still on him. His concern was not about the dread of his circumstances; he was not terrified by God; he wanted God to come down and explain his circumstances to him. His hope rested in who God was.

At the end of chapter 14, we find the last point Job made to Zophar. Hope was not in repentance or in death for the wicked; it was in God. The fourth point was that hope was not in man's accomplishments; it was not even based in time. Let us consider Job's thoughts in 14:18–21. He spoke of the deterioration of earth and God's control. He spoke of the events of life, family, and man's lack of understanding. He acknowledged none of these things could bring hope. Job's hope was in God. He did not rely on the accomplishments of time. His foundation for hope was not in what he or his children had done. He knew in time the earth would wash away. He knew that on earth, in our time frame, things were going to happen. In our death, we were not going to know whether it was good or bad. Therefore, our hope could not be placed in time, nor could it be placed in accomplishments, either ours or our children's. Hope was in God.

Parents too often live vicariously through their children. They were not able to accomplish their dreams, so they push their kids to achieve. This is nothing new; this is what Job was addressing. Whether his kids had done great things or lousy things was not going to matter. In terms of hope, it was not relevant. In terms of our future, neither what we nor our children do will make a difference. The mountains will fall and the rocks will move in time; we cannot place our hope in the actions or activities of time. Sometimes we work hard to achieve a goal, and I am not going to diminish either the efforts or the accomplishments because we need vision and goals. Funerals, however, bring perspective. Some say the deceased will be remembered forever and the feelings will last forever, but let us be honest. That is not going to happen. It is easy to feel that way in the emotion of the circumstances, but time teaches us otherwise.

In life, it is easy to feel that we are doing something that will last forever, that we are making a huge difference by our actions. When my youngest daughter was involved in ministry with a group of junior high and high school students, she talked about some changes that were happening. She was struggling with the idea she was making a huge difference in these kids' lives. I told her, "I know how important that feels. At the end of their lives, it will probably have made a difference. However, it will not nearly be as big as you think." I remember when I was her age. I was a junior high Sunday school teacher. I visited in their homes, trying to make a difference by investing in their lives. I would be willing to bet at this point not all of those kids could come up with my name. Time passes, and memories fade; Job understood this. Our hope cannot be based on the temporal activities of this or any other generation. Hope must be found in God, in the finished work of the cross. Hope is based on what God has done. Hope is found in the fact that there is a mediator who can place His hand on God and man. The wonderful song *The Solid Rock* captures this truth: "My hope is built on nothing less than Jesus' blood and righteousness." That is absolutely true. Jesus' blood and righteousness are the only sources of hope. Our hope has to be completely planted in the finished work of the cross, not our repentance, not our religious works, not our changed behavior.

Hope is the result of what Jesus has done for us. He died for the sins of the world, but our hope must rest on the fact He died for us. He resolved our separation from God, our sins, our falling short of His righteousness. The who of our hope, the what of our hope, the where of our hope needs to be answered in Jesus.

Job understood the source of his hope was in his relationship with God. When our hope is in Jesus, we cannot be shaken. Hope is in God. The circumstances of life can challenge our hope. People, events, and finances may be fickle, but this is why our hope must be built on nothing less than Jesus' blood and righteousness. Hope is in the unchanging, eternal provision of God. It was the anchor of God's champion, Job.

CHAPTER 9

The Wicked

Job 15:1–17:16

The study of Job is the study of God. It is not about suffering or failure. God had a champion in His battle with Satan; He initiated this challenge regarding His servant Job. God contended there was none like him (Job 1:8); Satan said Job would deny God if His blessing and protection were removed (Job 2:10, 11). God allowed that to happen, and Job was left destitute. His friends showed up to comfort him. After they had sat in silence, they began to take turns expressing their explanations of Job's condition. So far, we have considered the first speeches of Eliphaz, Bildad, and Zophar.

The context is particularly important as we explore Eliphaz's second argument. It will sound impressive, and we may find ourselves agreeing with him. Error is often wrapped in part of the truth. We will have to pay close attention to discover the skewed nature of Eliphaz's assertions in his second speech.

In the last chapter, we asked the question, "What is the basis of my hope?" We saw that hope was not in our repentance or any other religious behavior. A right relationship with God is never based on our behavior but on the finished work of Jesus. Second, we rejected Zophar's claim that hope was in death for the wicked. However, there is no hope in judgment for the wicked (Heb. 9:27). Death closes the door to hope. The opportunity to accept God's gift of eternal life ends. In God and God alone is hope. The last thing Job expressed at the end of his speech was that his hope was not in his accomplishments or things but in God.

This chapter is the second exchange with Eliphaz. Those who like sarcasm will certainly enjoy Job's response. Eliphaz had an attitude; he was worked up at that point. Eliphaz, Bildad, and Zophar had spoken, but Job had not responding to their counsel. Eliphaz was a little exercised that Job was so recalcitrant and had not embraced their wise counsel, and he seriously attacked Job in this exchange. Their conversation deteriorated from a nice Eastern style—you talk and I will listen, after which I talk and you will listen—to a fourth-grade level. I think a loose interpretation of this exchange would sound something like this.

"You started it."

"Did not."

"Did to."

"You're the wicked one."

"No I'm not. You are!"

That seems the nature of this conversation. Our focus in this chapter is, "Who are the wicked?" Eliphaz accused Job of being wicked and did not conduct his inquisition with any niceties. He came after Job with everything he had because Job had been unresponsive. He wanted to be very clear. The condensed version would be, "Job, you're a wicked man." No wonder God told Eliphaz he had not spoken well of Him as Job had (Job 42:7). It is reasonable in our consideration of the Creator to understand who is wicked. What is the real nature of wickedness? What does it look like? Eliphaz did not miss it by much. He just tweaked it a little bit and traveled in the wrong place; his minor alterations created the problems. We do not run around in outright failures; we tweak them just enough to wind up in error. Sadly, we may not even know it. We are so caught up in our own perceptions and our own assumptions that we miss the truth.

So who are the wicked? I think all would agree that Job 15:3 indicated that Eliphaz was on the right track. Read verses 1 through 3; they give our first answer to the question. The wicked are those who hinder the worship of God. I would assume we agree with Eliphaz's assertion. The wicked are those who cause others to flee from God's presence, to resist entering His presence, or to dampen enthusiasm for pursuing the things of God. These are not nice people, and Eliphaz stated this clearly. However, he applied this to Job. He contended that Job was keeping people from worshiping God. Because of this, Job needed to repent of his foolishness and get over himself; then everyone could get back to worshiping. The problem was with Eliphaz's concept of worship. He believed worship was doing the right thing rather than a relationship with God and entering into His presence.

Today, many people live in the same misunderstanding. They embrace behavioral Christianity. Jesus addressed behavioral Judaism (Matt. 22:23). We do the right things. We go to the right seminars, listen to the right music, go to the right places, attend the right denomination, and read the right Bible. However, each tends to have a different list. Some call other legalistic while creating their own rules of behavior. The problem is the same; the rules are different. We miss the fact that Christianity is a relationship with the living God who loved us and died for us. Does that mean we can do whatever we please? No, because in our relationship with God, He lives in us (Gal. 2:20). We learn how to behave in a fashion that becomes appropriate and meaningful.

Let me give a couple examples. Husbands and wives, when you said, "I do," did you really understand the person you married? Be honest! Say no. We grow into our understanding of our spouses by spending time with them. Because we love them, we get to know them. We learn to understand what they do and do not like, what they do and do not do. We learn to modify our actions and expectations because we love them. As we grow in our relationship and understanding, we willingly change because we love them, we want to please them, and we want to share our lives with them. We need to do the same thing with God. We need to build a relationship with God, the very reason He created us. Some people wonder, "What was I created to do?" That question has many answers. However, there is one primary answer from Scripture: you and I were created to walk with God (Gen. 3:8, 5:22, 6:9). That is what He did with Adam and Eve. God created us for relationship with Himself. We need to pursue Him and respond to His pursuit of us because He desires relationship with us.

Eliphaz completely failed in his argument. If God desired relationship, then how the worship of God is hindered becomes a different discussion. I agree with Eliphaz about those who hinder the worship of God, those who diminish our desire to love Him with our whole heart. However, worship is not based on who we are, where we go, or what we do; worship is based on what Jesus has done for us. It is based on our hearts' relationships with Him. As I have a thriving relationship with God, I will repent of my sin. I will change my behavior. I will stop doing the things that offend others. Out of my love relationship with God, His Spirit will change me. Gal. 2:20 tells us, "It is no longer I who live, but Christ lives in me." If He is living His life in me, I am being transformed. I cannot continue being who I am while being in love with Him. I could not continue being who I was and in love with my wife. I am not the person she married. We can agree with Eliphaz's statement but disagree with his analysis.

Eliphaz gave his second view of Job's wickedness a few verses later. Look at verses 9 and 10. "What do you know that we do not know? What you understand that we do not? Both the gray-haired and the aged are among us, older than your father." Eliphaz believed that those who reject the wisdom of experience were wicked. I think we would temper his conclusion by calling them "foolish." Those who reject the wisdom of experience are destined to repeat mistakes. You have heard the adage, "The one thing we learn from history is that we do not learn from history." People reject the wisdom of experience; they have been doing it for a long time. Eliphaz made a true point: rejecting the wisdom and understanding of those who came before us and repeatedly making the same mistakes are at best foolishness and may be wicked. Everybody knows someone who operates that way. You may be that somebody, or you may have children who seem obligated to make mistakes for themselves rather than learn from the experience of others. They cannot grasp the concept that the same actions were mistakes for everyone else. I do not understand that thinking, or lack of thinking. In junior high and high school, I saw the heartache of guys and girls getting together and breaking up and doing it over and over. I did not want that pain in my life. I could smell the stale stench of tobacco and did not want to spread the odor. I was not righteous or self-willed to do the right thing; I created my own problems. However, I could watch and learn. I praise God for His grace in my life. He kept me from multiple mistakes.

Eliphaz was mistaken, not on the point that it is wicked or at least foolish to reject the wisdom of experience but on his analysis of the facts. This was evident in the question he asked: "What do you know that we do not know?" There was something Job knew that they did not. He knew he had a right standing before God. He knew God was his advocate. He knew God's hand was still on him. He did not have an explanation for the circumstances of his life. He knew he was not wicked; he knew he was not rejecting the wisdom of those who had come before him. Eliphaz was having trouble with the application of what he knew to be true. We have the ability to do that as well. Our analysis is good. We understand the truth. We understand how things work. What we do not understand is what God is doing in other people's lives. We analyze their lives and commit the same mistake as Eliphaz. We do not know what God is doing in their lives any more than Job knew what God was doing in his.

Have you ever felt like that? Have you ever asked, "God, what are you doing in my life? I don't understand." You find other people willing to help with crazy answers, and they usually have the same kind of advice as Job's friends had: it is because you are sinning, and if you repent, everything will get back to normal. Have you ever experienced such help from friends? They are arrogant and clueless but do not know it. We do not want to reject the wisdom of experience. In doing analysis, we need to understand the principles of life. If we do not, we may become the wicked person of Eliphaz's concern.

The wicked are those who hinder the worship of God and reject the wisdom of experience. Eliphaz came to his third point in verses 11 through 16. He contended that nothing was pure enough for God. Eliphaz said God was not happy or satisfied with anything or anybody. He did not like what He had created. He did not like people and did not trust His angels; they were all corrupt. From a story perspective, this is a good reason way God was not happy with Eliphaz. Everything created was corrupt before God.

The early church had to address this same problem. Everything spiritual was good and eternal; everything created was temporal and evil. This leads to very unbiblical places. For those who like philosophy, this clearly relates to some of the precursors of Platonic dualism. This concept holds that everything physical is evil but everything spiritual is good. We see that value in the church today. What is spiritual is good; what is physical is evil. Everything bad is from Satan; everything good is from God. While God allowed Satan to act, He took personal and direct responsibility.

What was created is good. On every day in the account of creation (Gen. 1), God said, "It is good." On a couple of days it was real good. One of those days was when He created man. God does not reject His angels or humanity. He values your life and your relationship. God loves you so much that He allowed Jesus to step out of eternity and into time to be abused and crucified. If you ever feel you are not good enough, remember you were good enough to justify Jesus dying for you. Eliphaz was completely mistaken about who God is. In a discussion of the wicked, he was on the wrong side. He declared everything created was wicked. Absolutely not! Job understood he was not wicked. God said of Job, "Behold my servant, there is none like him." God accepted Job, but his friends did not understand this fact.

Regarding those who hinder worship and those who reject the wisdom of experience, we can agree with Eliphaz on principle, not on merit. Regarding those who are created, we cannot go down that road because it does not agree with Scripture. He misunderstood. The logic of his third point is built on the errant assumptions of the first two. His fourth point is built on the third argument; we find it in verse 20: "The wicked man writhes in pain all his days, and numbered are the years stored up for the ruthless." Eliphaz went point by point to establish that the wicked suffer and were punished. They did not have money or friends. He made errant statements verse after verse and was totally wrong. However, it was clearly built on the assumption that those who were created were evil, rejected, and had to be punished. The wicked experienced retribution poured out on them by God. From Eliphaz's frame of reference, it was self-evident that Job was wicked. He was suffering! No further proof was necessary because God punished the wicked.

According to Eliphaz, if you are suffering, it is because you are a bad person, and there are Christians who accept Eliphaz's logic. Turn to Micah 4:6: "'In that day,' declares the Lord, 'I will assemble the lame and gather the outcast, even those whom I have afflicted.'" Here and elsewhere in Scripture, God takes personal responsibility for the grief in our lives. I am not happy about that. Nevertheless, I see that is what God declares. It is not because we have been bad. It is not because God is trying to make a point. For most of us, this is the question we want answered at the end of Job, when God shows up. However, He does not answer the questions, "Why did Job suffer? Why did Job experience all of this? Why did Job experience grief and loss? Why was Satan allowed to take everything away?" We never get an answer. We, like Job, have to rely on who God is. How did Job respond? "Though he slay me, I will hope in Him" (Job 13:15). "The Lord gave and the Lord has taken away. Blessed be the name of the Lord" (Job 1:20). That is faith, commitment, a love relationship with the King of kings.

Chapter 16 is Job's reply. It expresses his frustration and hope. He felt abandoned and expressed his broken heart. In verse 11 he said, "God hands me over to ruffians and tosses me into the hand of the wicked." This expression underscores the importance of remembering that Job spoke what was right about God. His confidence was in the Lord. That is where we need to live.

I marvel at Job's ability to stand in the grace of God, believe he knows God, and have a relationship with Him without the support of friends or family. He was sure of his place in the presence of God. Typically, we do not have to struggle with the lack of support. If we are struggling, some will come alongside us and encourage us. There are those in the body of Christ who will love us unconditionally. That is how you know you are in the right church. If you do not have those who support you through trials, go somewhere else. The body of Christ needs to be an encouraging group of people who love one another unconditionally through our challenges, failures, and frustrations. Human beings struggle (1 Cor. 10:13). There are times when we desperately need the embrace of our brothers and sisters in Christ. We need reminders that God is in control, that He loves us, and that we will be victorious (Phil. 4:13). Sometimes we may not want to hear it, but we still desperately need it. That is who we are in our humanity, even when we are trying to be strong and think we can handle it. Loving others is the hallmark of Christianity (John 15:35).

I can think of Christians I have visited in hospitals or those who knew they were dying. Their faith gave them strength, but their humanity gave them concern. Some chose to chide them for their lack of faith; others understood the need to support them. Your brothers and sisters in Christ need to be encouragers, not critics. Ask yourself, "Whom did Jesus criticize even in their failures?" Not the woman at the well

(John 4). Not the women caught in adultery (John 10). Not Nicodemus (John 3). Not Zaccheus (Luke 19). Not even Peter. He was encouraged to "tend my lambs" (John 22:15). Christ prayed for him.

We all need the embrace of other people when we struggle. When we are dealing with personal, family, financial, or emotional issues, we need the encouragement and support of others. We have all been there. When there are clouds over us, we need the embrace of the body of Christ. God is at work. We need those who will listen and encourage. None of us needs to be judged for our struggles; God's grace is sufficient. Job could walk with God, and so can we. We need one another and the assurance of Job regarding God's grace.

Job knew he was not wicked. He did not hinder the true worship of the God he knew. He knew he did not reject the true wisdom of previous generations. He knew what God created was not wicked. He also knew his suffering did not make a statement about his relationship with God. Job had spoken what was right about God like a champion.

CHAPTER 10
My Redeemer Lives
Job 18:1–19:29

This chapter brings us to the fifth exchange between Job and his friends and the second encounter between Bildad and Job. Before discussing each of these exchanges, we should remind ourselves of the facts. God had asked Satan, "Have you considered my servant Job? There is no one like him" (Job 1:8). At the end of the story, God held the same opinion. He told Eliphaz, "You and your friends have not spoken what is right of me like my servant Job" (Job 42:7). No matter how convincing Job's friends may be, they are wrong.

Job was the hardest book I have ever tackled for preaching. A major factor in the difficulty was the constant need to wrap my mind around who were the good guys and bad guys. I start with a reminder of what God said for my benefit as well as the readers'. To represent God accurately, I need to keep the issues straight. God's analysis requires us to look carefully at what Job's friends were saying. We need to grapple with the ideas and understand why God was offended. I should not flirt with what offends God. Have you wondered if Job was an example through his whining and complaining? I think David, a man after God's heart, took lessons from Job. Some of the psalms whine and complain; the author wants God to kill all his enemies (Ps.143:12), make sure their children are fatherless, and turn their homes into ash heaps (Ps.110:9–10). Jonah was not pleased with God's decision to spare Nineveh and said so. Jeremiah is called the weeping prophet. God's perspective and cultural differences should give us reason to temper our concerns about Job's approach.

Before we dissect this exchange between Bildad and Job, let us summarize the last chapter. Eliphaz raised the question of who the wicked were and accused Job of being wicked. We saw and would agree that those who hinder the worship of God are not nice. Second, Eliphaz accused Job of rejecting the wisdom of experience, but then he moved beyond reasonableness by saying everything created was evil. His last argument was that everything spiritual was from God and everything physical was bad and from Satan. That does not represent the God of the Bible or biblical values; creation is not evil. Eliphaz also declared that everyone who suffered was wicked. Biblically, there was something wrong with his analysis.

It was then Bildad's turn to explain to Job why he was suffering. He perceived that Job was not repenting of his failures and continued to cling to his foolishness. He obviously agreed with Eliphaz that Job was wicked and wanted a turn to make the argument. Bildad made the observation in Job 18:5–14 that the wicked lack character and claimed in verses 15–17 that those who lost their personal and material possessions were wicked. Further, he stated they were going to be rejected by God.

Bildad logically concluded from his assumptions that Job and been rejected by God because he had lost all his material and personal possessions. Since these things would not have happened if he had been a man of character, it was self-evident that Job was not such. He suggested that Job just get over himself and repent, the appropriate action for a wicked person.

The question I want us to consider in light of Bildad's condemnation is, "Where do we find our confidence?" We probably have experienced devastating situations that have left us quivering in the corner. Hopefully, our experiences were more figurative than factual, but sometimes life's difficulties push us so far out of our comfort zone that we struggle to maintain any semblance of control. We become overwhelmed by problems, circumstances, or relationships and find ourselves at a loss to figure out the right direction or decision. We might be hoping for options, any options, and fear that there is no reasonable outcome. Life is a struggle if not a nightmare. At that point, we understand where Job was living and gain a little insight into his feelings. He had lost his family, his possessions, and his health. He seemed to be losing even his friends and was asking why God had allowed this to happen. Job's life was incredibly difficult. How do we begin to understand or identify with his circumstances? Nevertheless, everyone has or will experience tough places in life.

So back to the question we want to answer: "What was the anchor that empowered Job to maintain his sanity?" When we struggle for orientation because life seems to be spinning out of control, we need a source of permanence, an anchor of stability, a foundation for our confidence that provides proper orientation. We need to stand in the security of knowing, as Job did, that our Redeemer lives.

Bildad told Job that he had problems because of an obvious lack of character. He had lost all his possessions because God had rejected him. What else did Job need? Job had been kicked to the curb by his friends. Maybe you have felt like that right when you needed a source of security or confidence. So let us consider the basis of Job's confidence. His first three responses were areas that do not provide security in his relationship with God. He knew they would not withstand the storms of life. He challenged Bildad's comments by asserting that the issues he raised did not matter. Job told his friends to get off their high horses. In Job 19:2, Job loosely said, "How long will you guys torment me? Don't you see my grief? I don't need your condemnation. How long are you going to crush me with your words? At least ten times you've insulted me. Aren't you ashamed of your inaccurate condemnations?" In verse 7 he said,

> Behold, I cry violence but I get no answer; I shout for help, that there is no justice. He has walled up my way so that I cannot pass, He has put darkness on my paths. He has striped my honor from me and removed the crown from my head.

Job claimed God had acted to remove the appearance of his character. The problem is with the perception of others. This understanding comes from the Eastern terms used of "light" and "darkness." There is content in the idea of having the crown removed from one's head. These are symbols in the Eastern thinking that were prevalent in these exchanges that said that Job had no value. He was viewed as a person without character. He said that he understood their argument but that they did not understand the issues. Remember, Job spoke what was right about God even if we are a little uncomfortable with his expressions.

Verse 11 reads, "He has also kindled his anger against me and considered me as his enemy. His troops come together, and build up their way against me and camp around my tent." That is a difficult place to be. Job did not disagree with Bildad's perception of his condition but challenged him on the cause. Job countered that he was not counting on his character because God had changed his circumstances and altered the perception of those around him. Job declared he was not counting on his integrity.

The book of Romans, chapters 2 and 3, makes the point that all are sinners. Many know Romans 3:23, "For all have sinned and fall short of the glory of God." Paul spent most of his letter to verse 23 building his argument so that nobody would miss it. He established that the bad guys were sinners, the good guys were sinners, and the religious guys were sinners. Everyone was a sinner. Job understood the biblical condition of man, including himself. He was not counting on his personal integrity or righteousness because neither made a difference to God.

If you have had much interaction with non-Christians, you know that many say they are good enough to get to heaven. They often make comparisons that if so-and-so, who claims to be a Christian, is good enough to get into heaven, then they are as well. People want to count on their personal integrity or righteousness. Some will say they keep the Ten Commandments, but if you ask them to list the ten, they may not get even to one. They can be clueless. Nevertheless, one approach or the other, they reveal that they are counting on their personal righteous to get them to God.

Personal integrity is a good thing. I am not suggesting we behave like sinners because it does not matter, it is all under the blood. Nevertheless, our integrity or righteousness is not going to be the basis of our standing before God. Job understood this truth. He told Bildad that accusing him of a lack of integrity did not matter. Job understood he had fallen short of God's standards, but so what? How did that matter? Job was not relying on his integrity but his relationship with God.

At verse 13, we see Job's second characteristic that will not be a source of strength when life is uncertain. For some like Job, it is an additional source of conflict. Job did not find this to be a refuge, an anchor of security, or a source of stability in his life. He said, "He has removed my brothers far from me, and my acquaintances are completely estranged from me. My relatives have failed, and my intimate friends have forgotten me." Some people rely on their families to be their anchors and expect to count on them in times of trials and difficulties. However, we know it is not always true; many of us have learned this by experience. We need to have an anchor securely placed where it will keep us properly oriented in life.

Regarding family, let us remind ourselves of Jesus' words to his followers that unless they were willing to forsake (hate) father and mother, brother and sister, son and daughter, they were not worthy to follow Him (Luke 14:26). Jesus is not advocating the denial or rejection of familial responsibilities or relationships, but family cannot be our anchor; it cannot be what guides and directs our lives. Families may not be the force that keeps us on the straight and narrow because they can fall short.

Joseph had the same dad as his brothers. Absalom had the same dad as Solomon. Cain had the same parents as Abel. We know, whether as parent or child, there are things we should have done but did not, and things we should not have done but did. We have offended our children and have been offended by our parents. This applies to those with whom we work, and it could apply to neighbors and friends. If we are counting on the goodwill of family, we may find ourselves being tossed about without any security.

Job said he had lost it all. While Bildad lumped together possessions and family, Job separated them. He moved from his family to his friends in verse 19: "All my associates abhor me." He had lost his friends. At that point, his friends were not there to support him. Individuals are sometimes driven by the desire to have others think well of them and let the opinions of others direct their lives. They want the people around them to speak and think well of them; if that happens, life is good; they feel needed, and life has meaning. When they question what they did or others are not happy with them, they have a bad day. We cannot orient our lives by the compass of other people's opinions. We will never find the security necessary to anchor our lives in the midst of trials and chaos in the opinions of others. Friends are nice to have, but we cannot use them as anchors, as strength, when life becomes chaotic. They may not be able to help us get through tomorrow. It is nice if they do; but our anchor needs to be elsewhere. Our friends, like Job's friends, may say, "See you later; we do not agree with you." Job's friends told him the problems he experienced were because he was a bad person, and that will not work as an anchor in uncertainty.

I have had that experience, and you may have also. When I was in seminary, my closest friend worked with me to change my conversation. I was a negative, critical person. He helped me express thankfulness and supportive statements. At one point, I was supposed to call him every day with at least one positive thing I had said, but there were days I could not think of even one. He worked with me to change my thinking and verbal expressions. I valued his relationship highly. I knew the importance of the change he helped facilitate in my life. Unfortunately, one day he told me I was rebellious, disloyal, and immoral. He was wrong on all three accounts; if his opinion had been my anchor, I would have been blown away. Fortunately, my anchor was somewhere else. David said, "Even my close friend in whom I trusted, who ate my bread, has lifted up his heel against me" (Ps. 41:9). We need friends in our lives, but they cannot be the place we anchor our souls.

Job made some of the most incredible statements to his friends. He had an anchor to hold even though his friends told him he was not a man of integrity. Job said it did not matter because he knew that was not the basis of his spiritual standing with God. They told Job that because he had lost everything he must be wicked. Job responded it did not matter. His friends attacked him because he had lost his family and possessions. Job declared it did not matter. He knew his anchor was not in wealth, health, family, or friends (Job 1:21). In verse 25, he revealed the anchor of his soul, the reason he could bless the Lord in spite of the circumstances. "As for me, I know that my Redeemer lives, and at the last He will take His stand on the earth. Even after my skin is destroyed, yet from my flesh I shall see God" (Job 19:25–26). The joy of this anticipation kept him anchored. He did not allow his circumstances and conditions to be a distraction to his relationship with God.

Job turned the table on them in the last couple of verses by asserting that there was no case against him and that those who persecuted him were bringing punishment upon themselves. He told Bildad he was on the wrong side of the issues because his Redeemer lived. He was not relying on his experiences in the here and now. He was aware that he was going to die, that his flesh would be destroyed. Yet he knew that with his eyes he would see God (19:26). Job had a sound theology. It is amazing the things he understood. Job gave us clarity about the God we worship.

Let us expand on what he understood about God. Job understood that his Redeemer was alive and would someday rule and reign on earth. We understand Jesus is coming to rule and reign on the earth (Rev. 21:1–4). We understand Jesus came, died, and was resurrected. Job understood he would be alive in his flesh. He did not have all the details, but he clearly grasped the outcome. Job understood he was going to be resurrected, and he anticipated a bodily, physical resurrection. It was with his eyes that he would see God (Job 19:25–26). He also understood God was a God of judgment. Job never challenged that God would judge or punish the poor behavior his friends described. He understood the importance of not being on the wrong side and warned his friends (Job 19:29). He knew his Redeemer was a God of judgment. This is affirmed later when God speaks to Eliphaz: "You are in trouble because you have not spoken well of me" (Job 42:7 paraphrased). Job spoke accurately of God. He knew because of his relationship with his Redeemer he would be blessed, maybe not in the here and now, but in the future.

That is the place where we can anchor our soul, find peace in turmoil, the peace Jesus promised, and build certainty. Jesus told His disciples, "Peace I leave with you; My peace I give to you; not as the world gives do I give to you" (John 14:27). We can have peace when our soul is anchored in our living Redeemer, knowing He is a just judge, knowing we will be blessed, and knowing we have eternal life. Peace or judgment is the choice. When chaos is swirling in our lives and nothing is making sense, we need anchor for our souls. The turmoil may be physical; it may involve the loss of things, a job, or a family, or it could be due to a misunderstanding. Any of these can cause chaos in our lives. We need an anchor, and our anchor needs to be a living Redeemer.

God has made provision for peace. His people will continue to rely on their integrity, count on their families, and seek security in friends and possessions. But the anchor that holds us secure in chaos is a living Redeemer and a relationship with Him.

So where is your confidence in life and death? That is the most important question we answer. If you do not know Jesus, do you want to? It is easy. It is a relationship with Jesus. You recognize that like Job you deserve God's punishment. You accept that Jesus' death on the cross paid the penalty for your sins. You give Him the right to live His life in you and thank Him for making you a child of God. There are no special words or magic ceremonies. It is the new birth Jesus told Nicodemus about (John 3:3). If you know your Redeemer, you still face the same issues, turmoil, and chaos. Is He your anchor, or are you going to face life in your own strength? Are you going to rely on your possessions and family? Are you going to walk in your own competence and integrity? The alternative is a living Redeemer. Even after being accused by his friends, suffering from ill health, losing wealth and family, Job could say his Redeemer lived. Job was a true champion. His confidence was amazing. He was anchored in the peace and the provision of God. God will hold us secure through all the challenges of life, every day.

CHAPTER 11
Guarding Our Hearts
Job 20:1–21:34

The book of Job is not about suffering. Oh, there is plenty of suffering in it! Job whined and complained. We previously asked in chapter 5 if it was all right to complain and concluded it was. Job certainly did. God said, "Job spoke what was right of Me" (Job 42:7). God has invited us into His presence, and not just when we have good things to say and are excited about life. He has invited us into his presence even when we are not happy about life. Things are happening that need God's touch, grace, and mercy. Unfortunately for us, God feels no compelling need to explain the whys of our experiences.

The last chapter was the second encounter between Job and Bildad. We asked, "What is the basis of our confidence?" Job said he was not counting on his personal integrity, though He affirmed he had done what was right. He was not counting on his family or friends. He had confidence, which rested in his Redeemer, to face the circumstances and trials of life.

This is a book about God, not Job. God and Satan were engaged in a spiritual battle, and Job was God's champion. God believed Job would validate the value of a relationship with Him that did not rely on benefits provided—health, wealth, or family. At the beginning, God said there was no one like him

(Job 1:8), and the end, He told Eliphaz that he and his friends had not spoken what was right of Him (Job 42:7). It is our responsibility to wrap our minds around God's perspective. Remember that it is important to hold God's perspective even when listening to or reading godly men.

As we come to Job chapter 20, we read Zophar's second speech, so I encourage you to read chapters 20 and 21. You will see that Zophar, who was upset, confused emotion with reason. You may recall that in the previous chapter Job said they were not doing well in their analysis. He also cautioned them to be very careful about their judgments because judgment was coming and could be on them. As a result, Zophar was not happy. He was worked up, maybe angry, and said he had to speak. Experience may have taught us that when we feel compelled to speak, we should probably keep our mouths shut and our thoughts to ourselves because we may be confusing emotions with the Spirit's promptings; God may not be leading. The truth is that we are not happy; we are taking up an offense; we are frustrated by what is happening.

Zophar's second problem is explained in the book of James, in which we learn to be quick to hear and slow to speak (James 1:19). We can tell Zophar had been thinking about what he was going to say while Job was speaking and had not been listening. Have you ever found yourself doing that? I have. Zophar illustrated what happens when our mouths are engaged but our brains are two feet behind. When your thoughts are struggling to catch up with your mouth, the result can be ugly, and this is what Zophar was doing. In his zeal to speak, Zophar, like his friends, advocated a cause-and-effect spirituality. Sadly, this is common today; it is so deeply ingrained in our humanity that it dies hard. You do what is right, you get blessed; you do what is wrong, you have problems. Zophar reminded Job he had lost his family and his wealth and was suffering physically; because these were serious problems, it was obvious to Zophar that Job was wicked, but if Job got his act together, God would bless him.

That is cause-and-effect spirituality, and too many wish it worked that way. The book of Job is the best place to learn that it is not a biblical position. We see Zophar doing what we all do. The Bible tells us people look on the outward while God looks at the heart (1 Sam. 16:7). Zophar was looking at the outward, at what happened, the losses and the struggle, at Job's trials and apparent failure. God was looking at the heart of Job and knew the relationship they had. At the end of the story, God said that Job had spoken what was right about Him. Zophar had not; he had a problem with the wicked and the punishment of the wicked. As you read through his speech, you will see he compared the wicked to dung and to a dream. Zophar thought the wicked would eventually disappear; in judgment, the wicked just go away. We will see later in Job there is judgment coming for everyone. Zophar was mistaken. He also claimed that even if our wickedness was not punished in our lifetime, our kids would be punished. That is not biblical. I cannot blame Adam, the devil, or anybody else. Judgment is not passed down. We are individually responsible and cannot blame another (Rom. 1:20, 3:23).

Some commentaries supported this argument by Zophar. They drew that conclusion because the Old Testament states that the sins of the parents are passed on to the third and fourth generation (Ex. 20:5, 34:7) and conclude that was God's judgment. I would say it is the natural consequence of behavior. Sins and judgment are not the same. We will all experience judgment for our sins. The previous generation gave them permission to act or they created a favorable environment, but that is not God moving judgment down to the next generation. Each generation deals with the results of their own choices. While we are sinners judicially (Rom. 5:19), we are sinners behaviorally by choice (Rom. 3:23). It seems wiser to apply the repeated contention that a parent or child does not pay the consequences for the other's acts (Deut. 27:3; 2 Kings 14:6; 2 Chron. 25:4). Judgment was not to be the result of what another did.

We saw the results of choice on both sides of an issue in the mid-twentieth century. The result of World War II provided unparalleled freedom for generations, while others made choices that created tyranny for generations. However, each generation has to protect or reject what it has been given. The consequences are results of their decisions. Let us be careful not to be confused about who represented God. Zophar was off base, as were Eliphaz and Bildad.

The questions I want us to answer in this chapter are, "How do we guard our hearts when people are condemning us with bogus claims? How do we handle being unjustly accused?" We know that we are right with God, that God has spoken to our hearts. We know we have done what we should have done. Job knew he was in right relationship with God, but everything in his life based on a cause-and-effect spirituality said that God was out to get him. His friends were condemning him, which was tough. I shared in the last chapter what I experienced in college and seminary with a friend who had invested significantly in my life but ultimately told me I was rebellious, disloyal, and immoral. I skipped the part about a whole group of people agreeing with him. Such a confrontation was a bit challenging. How do we survive in that situation? How do we continue as Job did? Where do we find the ability to guard our hearts like champions?

As you look through the next several verses, you will learn Job's source of strength. You should find these beneficial when challenged. Job told his accusers in verse 3, "Bear with me that I may speak; then after I have spoken, you may mock." That was an honest though not comforting expression. In verse 27 he said, "Behold, I know your thoughts, and the plans by which you would wrong me." First, if we are going to guard our hearts when unjustly accused, we must know our accusers are, how they think, and their frames of reference. Knowing what they are doing protects us from our own foolishness. Job knew they were going to mock him, so when they did, he was ready. He knew they planned evil against him, but he was ready for that. When we know our accusers and how they think, we can protect ourselves. If we think about those who have been our accusers in the past, we realize that what they did was not a surprise. Maybe we were a little surprised, but more significantly, we were probably disappointed. If we are going to guard our hearts, if we are going to walk in God's peace, if we are going to enjoy His presence, we must know our accusers.

One thing we know about ourselves and others is that we are human. As human beings we are going to misspeak, make mistakes, and offend. We will fall short of perfection. We know this about ourselves and are okay with our shortcomings. We want other people to be okay with our failures, but we do not want to be okay with theirs. We want them to do what is right and become upset when they do not.

Jonah illustrated this point. He knew that God was gracious and compassionate (Jonah 4:2) and that He had been so with Israel (Ex. 34:4–7). He knew God had been gracious with him when he had been tossed overboard in the middle of a storm (Jonah 1:15). However, when it came to Nineveh, he wanted God to rain down judgment (Jonah 3:10–4:1). Jonah was okay with his own lack of obedience, but when it came to others' lack in this respect, he demanded judgment.

Let us know our accusers and understand their humanity and their shortcomings, failures, and strengths. We who are husbands and wives understand this; we have to work at our relationships or our marriages fail. We are not perfect, but as Christians, if we work with the power and presence of God, He will allow us to adjust and change. We learn to be loved and to love in spite of our shortcomings. Knowing our accusers guards our hearts and protects us from what we know they will do.

The second truth is in Job 21:16. Job declared in the last half of that verse, "The counsel of the wicked is far from me." We need the counsel of the wicked to be far from us if we are to guard our hearts. We need to be very careful we are getting wise counsel in difficult circumstances. The wicked will suggest a variety of plans children of God have no business taking. Psalm 1:1 tells us, "Blessed is the man who does not walk in the counsel of the wicked, nor stand in the path of sinners, nor sit in the set of the scoffers!" We should not take counsel from people who have an anti-God perspective; they do not have a proper view of life and biblical values. If we listen to people who give us bad counsel, who are wicked, who do not see life from God's perspective, and who cannot bring godly wisdom to the table, they will fire up the emotions that want to do what is wrong. We are fighting that battle already when we have accusers attacking us, so we do not need any encouragement to fail. In our flesh, we want to lash back, to justify ourselves. We want to condemn them and explain why they have no idea about what they are talking. Of course we have tried that and know it does not work. It is important that we avoid bad counsel when we deal with the challenges of unjust accusers. We do not need any help doing what is wrong because we do that well enough on our own. We need wise counsel that will encourage us to walk in the power and presence of God and help us endure what is unjust, unfair, and, unreasonable.

We can find the third concept that will help if we desire to guard our hearts under accusation in Job 21:22. Job asked, "Can anyone teach God knowledge, in that He judges those on high?" Job was aware God was God and was willing to submit to His authority and control. On the other hand, he was unwilling to tell God what He needed to do or how God should have corrected what was happening. He was not going to substitute his wisdom for God's regarding what should be happening. Job raised the issue because of Zophar's assumptions regarding God's treatment of the wicked (Job 20:29). The obvious answer to Job's question of whether anyone can teach God knowledge is no; it just does not stop us from doing it. Too often we go to God with our lists of how He can make life better and explain the changes necessary with some person or circumstance; we imply or outright declare that if God would get involved, things would go much better for us. Maybe we want to ask God to remove a particular person from our lives, maybe a boss, or a neighbor, or an in-law. If God would only act, we think, things would be peaceful and we could serve Him better.

We, however, need to submit to God, who is at work in our lives and those of the people around us. Telling God how He ought to work is a bad idea. If we are going to guard our hearts, we cannot be helping God out; He does not need it. He knows what He is doing. He needs our cooperation and submission, not our direction. If we know our accusers, if we avoid bad counsel, and if we submit to God, we are well down the road to guarding our hearts from unjust accusers.

The last concept Job teaches us about guarding our hearts from unjust accusers is in Job 21:30, in which he said, "For the wicked is reserved for the day of calamity; they will be led forth at the day of fury." Judgment is coming. However, it is God's judgment and in God's time. Paul tells us in Romans 12:19, "Leave room for the wrath of God." Judgment is not a do-it-yourself project. Nevertheless, we want to see God's righteous judgment on people. We want to make sure that they understand who God is and that they had it coming. In fact, we will shower it on them and help God out. If we want to guard our hearts, this attitude will take us down the wrong road. It is important that we look to the future and focus on what God is doing. We need to learn God's intentions. The wicked are made for the day of judgment; they are not objects for our frustration. They will glorify God. In judgment, God will be glorified. We do not like that because we want God to be glorified now and look good and just in the process. We want our reputations protected.

In the last chapter, we learned Job was not counting on his reputation. He knew he could not, and we need to learn that we cannot. Our reputation does not get us right standing before God. God will settle accounts in the future by distributing crowns of gold. Judgment and reward will take place then. The white throne judgment is coming as sure as the sunrise (Rev. 20:11–15). God will separate the righteous from the unrighteous. Those who love Jesus, who submitted to His authority, and who entered into the finished work of the cross will enjoy His presence forever. Those who do not know God will be separated and suffer eternal punishment.

We do not have to get involved with God's judgment now or in the future; it is God's job. God has given humanity and His children things to do, but judgment is not one of them.

To guard our hearts, we must look to the future and let God be God. Knowing our accusers, avoiding bad counsel, submitting to God, and looking to the future will help us walk through the unjust accusations in times of frustration. It does not matter if the struggle is spiritual, behavioral, or emotional; it does not matter if the failure is actual or perceptual. God wants to give us His peace, the peace of a champion.

Chapter 12

Resting in God

Job 22:1–24:25

As I prepared this chapter, I became more and more excited about the truths the life of Job demonstrated. I trust that by the end of the chapter you will be as excited about this passage as I was. I believe from Job's experience that we can gain insight into who God is, and it will be as marvelous and as unexpected as Job's declaration, "My Redeemer lives" (Job 19:25) or "Yet from my flesh I shall see God" (Job 19:26). These truths state an awesome understanding of Job's relationship with the living God. Here is the same kind of depth in Job's understanding of God and his relationship with Him. As we end this chapter, we will consider the life of Jesus Christ as He faced the cross. We will find the same truths with Job and with Jesus at the cross, and they will demonstrate why Job was God's champion. He grasped the fundamental nature of his relationship with God and could rest in it.

Job has no shortage of accusers. Satan stood first in line in the opening scene in heaven. God asked him, "Have you considered my servant Job?" (Job 1:8). Satan loosely responded, "Hey, You protect him—no big deal. Why should he not serve You?" (Job 1:9–10 paraphrased). God told Satan he could take away all Job's stuff, and Satan did, but Job did not live down to

Satan's expectations. So Satan has another conversation with God and received permission to inflict Job (Job 2:6). Job sat on an ash heap and scraped his oozing sores with broken pottery, in agony from head to foot. In spite of his circumstances and condition, he was God's champion and asked, "Shall we indeed accept good from God and not accept adversity?" (Job 2:10). His friends showed up to declare that if he got his act together, God would stop all of this. Let us add "supportive friends" to the list of things Job lost. Through his experiences Job proved God right and Satan wrong.

Eliphaz was obviously vexed. This was his third go-around with Job. Eliphaz made his point clear in Job 22:5: "Is not your wickedness great, and your iniquity without end?" He was seriously exercised with Job and at that point was not providing much in the way of friendship. He continued in verse 6 to accuse him of taking unnecessary pledges or guarantees; that was followed up with the accusation he had taken their clothes. In verse 7, he accused him of not being hospitable, and in their culture, that topped the list of evil behaviors. In the name of hospitality, people would welcome others into their homes, offer them protection, and provide them with food. Verse 9 talked about him ripping off widows and orphans and treating them inappropriately. With friends like that, who needs enemies?

Eliphaz did not, however, provide one shred of evidence any of this was true. In fact, if anything like this had been true, we would have a problem with our theology. God had said there was no one like him (Job 1:8). If that was commendable behavior on Job's part, we have the wrong god. If God holds the right values, at the very least He is not omniscient. Both are a problem. Eliphaz was totally out of line. There was no foundation for the accusation. Sadly this still happens.

Nevertheless, Job interacted with his friends and maintained his cool most of the time. Every now and then he got a little testy, but on balance he was at peace with God. He did not condemn God for anything. As we find ourselves in unfair and unreasonable circumstances, being falsely accused, how do we appropriately respond? Because of Job's calmness, I want us to answer the question, "How do we find peace with God?" Jesus offered peace to His disciples in the Upper Room: "My peace I give to you" (John 14:27). Peace is our goal at the end of this chapter. In the life of Job, we have a living example. Do you want that kind of peace? I do!

If we are going to have peace with God, our first concept is nonnegotiable. Look at Job 23:10. Job, in speaking of God said, "But he knows the way I take; when he has tried me, I shall come forth as gold." We must believe God has a goal in our best interests (Rom. 8:28). If we do not, we will never have peace with God and will be "tried" by Him and frustrated by our experiences (see Appendix C). Job believed God was in control of his life and knew what He was doing. Job believed that at the end of the process he would be a more valuable resource. When we have that view, when that informs the perspectives of our lives, we will be at peace with God.

Biblical history teaches us that God had a goal. In the fullness of time, Jesus came and was born (Gal. 4:4). We are told God manifests His Word at the proper time (Tit. 1:3). God never acts too soon or too late. We see in the book of Hebrews that many were expecting Jesus but did not recognize Him (Heb. 11). They thought that God was slow about keeping His promises (2 Pet. 3:8–9). God has goals in the best interest of you, me—all humanity—and they have been in operation and continue to unfold. We are a part of that process, just as Jesus was. God's most basic goal is simply stated by Paul: God wants all men to be saved and to come to a knowledge of the truth (1 Tim. 2:4). God loves us and desires to have relationship with us. It is not God's goal that we run in rebellion separated from Him or face the consequences of our poor decisions. He is in no hurry to judge (Ex. 34:4–7); He wants to draw us to Himself and has made provision to accomplish His goal. We know God is sending Jesus to come get us so we can be with Him (John 14:3).

When I preach funerals, sometimes I use a passage in Thessalonians that instructs us to "comfort one another with these words" (1 Thess. 4:18). Paul talked about Jesus coming back and our being gathered to him. Therefore, comfort one another. Jesus is coming back. God has a goal; we are in process. At the end of that process, God is doing something marvelous (Phil. 1:6). Job could be at rest because of his commitment to God's work, and so can we!

The next characteristic that Job illustrates is in Job 23:11–12a. He gave the facts regarding Eliphaz's accusations. "My feet have held fast to His path; I have kept His way and not turned aside. I have not departed from the commandment of His lips." If we are going to be at peace with God, we need to live in the certainty of our actions before God. We cannot challenge ourselves about what we did or did not do. We cannot debate whether we should have done more or less. We cannot diminish our standing before God by wondering if we somehow do not measure up. Job knew he had done what God had expected of him, and we need to live in the same confidence. Even when we do, there will be people who will attack us and our characters and actions, but a champion knows his standing with God.

You are probably familiar with the saying that you can make some of the people happy some of the time. I think you can make many people unhappy anytime. We do not have to do anything wrong to upset people and create accusers, but we cannot be focused on the naysayers or fear the opinion of people (Prov. 29:25). We need to focus on our faithful walk with Jesus and where he has placed us today. We need to be at peace with what God has called us to do. Job was not looking at what had happened twenty years earlier or what might happen twenty years from then; he was simply looking at his present and was certain he had walked where God had asked him to. When we can share that perspective, we will be at peace with God regardless of our circumstances.

If we know God has told us to do something but are not doing it, we may not find much peace. Peace was probably not a general characteristic of Jonah's life, at least not in God's call to Nineveh. God has a way of reminding us of His expectations, and you may have experienced some of them. You knew God wanted you to do something, say something, or go somewhere, but the problem was your resistance, your reluctance to do so. Hopefully, you were not very comfortable with your resistance. We should praise God for our discomfort. If we are going to be at peace with God, we need to know that today we are walking where He has directed.

A scene in Corrie ten Boom's book *The Hiding Place* illustrates this truth. The Germans were bombing the city where she and her sister, Betsy, were living. One evening, when the disturbance woke them, they went downstairs for a cup of tea and heard the bombs and air-raid sirens. They talked about the war and what was happening in the world. Eventually, the bombing stopped and the sirens ceased, so they returned to their bedroom, where they found a piece of shrapnel embedded in the pillow Corrie had earlier been resting her head on. Corrie, frightened, wanted to play "what if." As she was going on and on, her sister pointed out the only safe place was in the center of God's will.

To be at peace, we need to be comfortable with living where God has called us today. We cannot second-guess or condemn ourselves; we cannot play "what if" regarding what we should or should not have done. We can be at peace with God today. That does not say anything about the future or the past; it speaks only of being at peace with God today. God does not hold us accountable today for what He will expect of us tomorrow, nor does He hold us accountable for the failures of the past because Jesus has already paid the price. Paul said, "Forgetting what lies behind and reaching forward to what lies ahead, I press on toward the goal for the prize of the upward call of God in Christ Jesus" (Phil. 3:13–14). We can be at peace with God only when we are keeping His way today and doing what He asks today.

David had the same kind of frustrations in some of his experiences. They were obviously different from Job's but certainly no less challenging. Saul was an accuser and a chaser. Later, it was David's son. David had some challenging experiences. In Psalm 17, he pens regarding his relationship with God,

> You have tried my heart; You have visited me by night; You have tested me and You find nothing; I have proposed with my mouth that I will not transgress. As for the deeds of man, by the word of Your lips I have kept from the path of the violent. My steps have held fast to your paths. My feet have not slipped. (Ps. 17:3–5)

David, in the midst of his challenges and trials, made the same declaration, "I have done what You have asked me to do." He found peace with God in that confidence. David was not at peace with Saul and was not necessarily at peace with his army. They thought he should kill Saul (1 Sam. 24). Nevertheless, David had peace with God.

We find peace with God when we know He has a goal and is operating in our best interests. We find peace with God when we know we are walking where He has asked us to walk and treasure His word in our hearts. Job 23:12b says, "I have treasured the words of His mouth more than my necessary food." When we hold the Word of God dear and allow it to search our hearts and conform our lives to his will, we will be at peace with God. The Psalms tell us, "Your word is a lamp to my feet and a light to my path" (Ps. 119:105). Earlier in the same psalm we are told, "How can a young man keep his way pure? By keeping it according to Your word" (Ps. 119:9). Are we allowing the Word of God to be a light to our paths?

When I was growing up, I struggled with my mouth. I did not understand that God had a lot to say about life and how I should live, including what I said. I had no idea that Scripture, from Genesis to Revelation, spoke directly to the things that came out of my mouth. God is very concerned about how we communicate with other people, but I was clueless. God has a wealth of material about how we verbally communicate. I, like too many professing Christians, was living in a functionally deist view of God. He wound up the world, and life just happened.

One of the projects I undertook to change that was to accumulate verses that addressed the things that come out of one's mouth. It related to the idea in Romans 12:1 of "renewing" my mind. I needed to learn God's perspective and to recognize the practical importance of treasuring God's Word in my heart. I collected over 2,000 verses that addressed the tongue, the lips, conversation, and speech. (See Appendix D for a few of these.) God has a lot to say. As I treasured His words and developed His perspective, I began to see God at work in my life. I wanted to conform my life to His desires; I wanted to live in faithfulness to Him. If we are going to be at peace with God, we need to align our lives with His desires. As did the psalmist, we need to treasure God's Word in our hearts.

Job illustrated one more characteristic that produces peace with God. We have to be in submission to His control, not at odds with His decisions. I am not at peace with anybody with whom I am in conflict. If we want to be at peace with God, we have to be in submission to His control. That concept is developed in Job 23:13–16, specifically verse 14: "For He performs what is appointed for me and many such decrees are with Him." Job made the point that his circumstances are a result of God's decisions and that he was okay with what God has done; he was willing to submit to God's will and to humble himself under His mighty hand (1 Pet. 5:6). James 4:7 says, "Submit therefore to God. Resist the devil and he will flee from you. Draw near to God and He will draw near." Verse 10 says, "Humble yourselves in the presence of the Lord, and He will exalt you." God will exalt us as we humble ourselves in the presence of God. A significant aspect of humility is submission. We need to allow God to be God; a champion does.

Job had peace with God because he knew God had a goal in his best interest. Job knew he was keeping God's ways and walking where God had asked him to walk. He treasured God's Word in his heart and allowed His Word to shape his thinking and values. Last, he lived in submission to God's will for his life. When these four characteristics are in our lives, we will be at peace with God.

Job was not the only one to live at peace with God because of these values. Later in the Bible, we find that Jesus did also. Many are familiar with John 14:27, in which Jesus was speaking with the disciples in the Upper Room and facing the cross in a matter of hours. Jesus told the disciples, "Peace I leave with you; My peace I give to you; not as the world gives do I give to you. Do not let your heart be troubled, nor let it be fearful." Jesus was offering the disciples peace and was making the same offer to you and me. Jesus was going to live in this peace through the experience of the cross. It was the same peace Job knew.

Jesus was facing the cross in the garden when he prayed, "Father, let this cup pass from Me" (Matt. 26:39). He was not looking forward to what He was about to face, but He continued to pray, "Not as I will, but as You will." He knew there was a goal, a value on the other side of what he was about to experience. Regardless of the brutal treatment of His body, His death, His separation from God, He knew the goal of relationship with you and me was on the other side. He was willing to face all the grief because of the goal. He knew God had a goal on the other side of the circumstances and so could face them in peace (Heb. 12:2). Jesus knew the goal; Job had to believe it in faith. Are you glad you do not know what you are about to face?

Jesus knew He had kept God's ways and had walked where God had directed Him. After Jesus and the disciples left the Upper Room, He prayed in John 17: "I glorified You on the earth, having accomplished the work which You have given Me to do" (4), "The words which You gave Me I have given to them" (8), "I was keeping them in Your name ... and I guarded them" (12), "I also have sent them into the world" (18), and "I have made Your name known to them" (26). Jesus was recounting that He had done what the Father had asked. Jesus was a peace in the garden because He had walked where God had asked Him to walk.

Jesus treasured God's word. We see this demonstrated often in His life, particularly as He dealt with Satan. At the beginning of Jesus' ministry, Satan tempted Him (Matt. 4) by suggesting Jesus turn stones into bread. Later, he suggested that He cast Himself off the temple and be rescued by angels, which would create a following of many. Jesus, in His humanity, quoted Scripture in response to the temptations because He treasured and valued the Word of God; He knew its power. Because He treasured God's Word in his heart, He could be at peace in the garden.

Jesus knew how he had to live, what he had to experience, and what he had to do. Jesus was willing to submit to God's will, to go to the cross. Because of this, He could be at peace in the garden.

The living examples of Job and Jesus teach us how to live at peace in the circumstances of life. Jesus did not give the disciples just words; He gave them a living example of the peace they could have. If we know God has a goal in our best interest, if we walk where He asked us to, if we treasure His Word in our hearts, and if we are willing to submit our will to His, we will find peace the world does not know. God's champions can live at peace in a hostile world.

CHAPTER 13

Secure in Righteousness

Job 25:1–28:28

While preaching through the book of Job, I had to remind myself Job was right and his friends were wrong (Job 42:7). Some commentaries explain why Job's friends were right and Job did not get it. For them, Job was guilty. In that scenario, logic would require that Satan had won the bet with God and both were wrong regarding Job's character. God asked, "Have you considered my servant Job? For there is no one like him on earth a blameless and upright man" (Job 1:8). God chose Job as His champion and removed His protection, giving Satan the freedom to devastate Job's life.

If Job had fallen short of being a "blameless and upright man," Satan would have been right, and God would have been wrong; Job's friends would have been right, and Job would have been wrong. Job consistently declared that he was righteous and blameless before God, that he had not done anything to cause offense. God said Job spoke what was right of Him. I find it awkward that so many find fault with Job, an amazing man, God's champion.

We discussed Job's third encounter with Eliphaz in the last chapter. Eliphaz was insistent that Job was an evil man, had failed to behave properly, and was unrepentant. Under such withering accusations, we asked the question, "How do we find rest in God?" We learned from Job we could rest in God if we knew God had a goal. Job knew God had a plan for what was happening in his life. Second, we learned we can rest in God by keeping His ways. Job knew and declared throughout the book he had done what God had asked him to do. Third, Job said he could rest in God because he treasured God's Word. When we value God's instruction, we will rest in God. Last, Job stated he had submitted to God.

Bildad did not like what Job had to say, so he took a third turn to challenge Job. His speech in Job chapter 25 is only six verses long, and it will help to read them. It is an attack on humanity and an affirmation of the unapproachability of God. He claimed nothing was good enough for God and compared humanity to a maggot or worm.

Job spoke what was right; Eliphaz and his friends spoke what was wrong (Job 42:7). Some things in these verses are in conflict with who God is. The first three verses were a claim that God ruled by force and likened Him to a tyrant or dictator, a governmental structure that would have been the norm in their world. He claimed that God, who ruled with an iron fist, was the one in charge and would not relent. That God ruled by force had been a common thread throughout the arguments of Job's friends, but Job knew this was not true.

Bildad's second mistake was contending that humanity had no hope. Verse 4 claimed that people could not be just before God. Bildad did not have a way for individuals to be clean before God. All born of woman were in a hopeless condition. Third, in verses 5 and 6, he held a very dim view of humanity in general, comparing him to a maggot or worm. Bildad clearly did not understand God carved time out of eternity and created mankind for fellowship. God fashioned Adam from the dust of the earth and breathed life into him (Gen. 2:7). All humanity, you and I, have been created in the image of God. Job understood, but His friends did not. Maybe they just failed to integrate it into their thinking. Genesis 1:27

gives us the simple declaration, "God created man in His own image."

Bildad was offended by Job's claims about God. Bildad's negative view that God ruled by force and that human beings were as hopeless as a maggot led to his argument with Job. Bildad wanted to know what made Job think he was so special; Bildad clearly had a problem with his understanding of God and the nature of His relationship with man. This was another attempt to establish that Job was wicked and unrepentant. Bildad saw Job standing as a maggot before a ruthless, unrelenting God. Let us ask how Job knew he was not wicked. We find Job's response to Bildad in chapters 26 and 27, in which he clarifies why they should have known he was not wicked as he drew a contrast between a champion and a wicked person.

I love Job's response at the beginning of chapter 26. In verses 2 through 4, he loosely said, "What a help you are to the weak!" Job challenged Bildad's counsel, his insight, and his source of understanding. In the balance of chapter 26, Job magnified the awesomeness of who God was in contrast to Bildad's claim. Job's understanding of God in chapter 26 laid the foundation for his defense in chapter 27. Job's first distinction between himself and the wicked is in verses 1 through 6. Because of his relationship with God, Job was convinced God was the giver of life. Life did not just happen; it came from God as a result of His creative decision and action. When Job said the breath of God was in his nostrils (Job 27:3), he recognized life was from God, who controlled its start, continuation, and end. Regardless of his circumstances, he refused to condemn God or "mutter deceit" (Job 27:4). He maintained his righteousness and said he did not reproach any of his days (Job 27:6). He sounds like a champion.

While Job declared his commitment to the life-giving God, he accurately understood that the breath keeping him alive was from God and spoke to that fact. That is an awesome realization and will differentiate the righteous from the wicked. I remember a speaker talking about the issues of life and death who may have been drawing on this idea from Job. He joked regarding the wicked that at some point God would say, "That is enough; you do not get any more of My air."

Because we are immersed in life, we get caught up in our responsibilities, sometimes missing the details as well as the big picture. Work, family, community, house, friends, something else, or all of the above have captured our attention. One day fades into the next, and suddenly years have passed. In the regularity of normalcy, it is easy to lose perspective, especially of our involuntary actions such as breathing. I am really glad I do not have to think about breathing, a gift from God. Job was aware of this valuable gift, maybe because of his circumstances, and it was an awesome realization. As you sit and read this book, your life, your breath, is a gift from God; we have His breath in our nostrils. Circumstances did not dampen Job's appreciation for God's good gifts (James 1:17). Life, a continuing gift, is foundational to the relationship of a righteous individual with God, and this would not be a wicked person's perspective.

When we devalue or misunderstand God's gift of life, we start talking about human beings as a maggot, a worm. We have lost sight of the reality that life is a precious gift of God. We should hold a biblical belief that God is intimately involved in our prenatal development (Ps. 139:13). If we do not, we will lose sight of the joys, values, and benefits God has provided us. If our relationship with God is going to endure the hardships of life and distinguish us from the wicked, we must cling to the fact that life is a gift from God. When we remove God as Creator, we remove rational order and any hope of meaning. Life becomes the result of time plus chance. Any semblance of order is accidental and therefore has no meaning. By recognizing God as the giver of life, we open the door to discovering meaning and purpose; it explains His desire to have a relationship with us and lays the groundwork for the necessity of the cross. Jesus is the way, the truth, and the life (John 14:6).

Job's second point is that the wicked have rejected God. In distinction, Job took the opportunity to clarify his relationship with God in verse 10. He made the point that the wicked do not delight in God nor do they call on Him in every circumstance. His comments began at verse 7 and ran through the balance of the chapter. It had been the contention of Job's friends that God rejected the wicked. They had argued in general that human beings were wicked and therefore God had rejected them. Job had tried to communicate that they did not understand how a relationship with God worked. It was the wicked who had rejected God; Job's friends had it backwards. In the day of calamity, they would not call on God. When they died and realized there was no hope, they were not going to call on God. God will not hear them call because they had rejected God in life and would do so in death. You may not have considered it that way before.

The psalmist told us that the wicked say, "There is no God" (Ps. 10:4). In their very heart of hearts, they are not going to call on God. Maybe you have known some of these people; many have been exposed to church or Christianity all their lives. They say they do not need God. They may arrogantly declare that on their deathbeds maybe they will recognize a need for God. When it comes to the end of life, because they have lived without God, they will conclude they are still not interested. They are convinced that God either does not exist or does not care. The wicked in their hearts have rejected God. Nevertheless, God is there, pleading with them. This is illustrate in that beautiful painting in the Sistine Chapel of God reaching down to man, desiring a relationship with all humanity. He has gone out of His way to pursue us, but many still respond with indifference and rejection.

That brings us to the third distinction between Job and the wicked. Job declared that God was the provider for man. Chapter 28 can be divided into two sections. The first eleven verses deal with things hidden in the earth. He used phrases such as "they refine gold," "copper is smelted," "he sinks a shaft;" and "he overturns the mountains." These show the material provisions God created for man. Job also talked about plants growing in the earth. He told us God had placed and invested all this in the earth as treasures, as resources, for the benefit of man. For physical life, it was the earth that provided for humanity. People in an agrarian environment tend to be more conscious of forces outside their control. The earth, one way or another, provides the tangible necessities of life and the inanimate materials such as ores and minerals and the organic nutrients required by the food we eat. God, as Creator, placed hidden treasures in the earth we need to mine and harvest. This was obvious to Job, in contrast to the view of the wicked; it was an additional reason he knew he was not wicked.

He then transitioned from the tangible provision of God in the earth to the spiritual or intangible provision in verse 12: "Where can wisdom be found? Where is the place of understanding?" He used this connection to make the point that just as life's resources are hidden in the earth, the resources of spiritual life are also hidden. We need to search them out to find what God has provided for us. They are available. At the end of this section, Job 28:28 said, "And to man he said, 'Behold, the fear of the Lord, that is wisdom; and to depart from evil is understand.'" God has provided for us morally and spiritually. Wisdom, which is from God, is the source.

Understanding God's provision is significant in our relationship with Him and His desired relationship with us. Job knew he was a righteous man in spite of the contrary contention of his friends. Because of His relationship with God and the value he placed in Him as the giver of life, he knew that was not what the wicked would do. Life was a gift, a trust, from God. Job knew the wicked, not the righteous, had a problem with God. They had rejected God, while he had not.

The third proof Job provided to establish he was not a wicked person was his acknowledgment that God had provided for him and all mankind physically and spiritually. Job was not willing to relinquish his integrity and agree with his accusers. He understood who God was and what He had done; he knew the wicked did not share his perspective on the character and nature of God.

He had gotten foolish advice from early in the story. His wife had counseled him, "Curse God and die!" (Job 2:9). If it was a bad idea from her, it is still a bad idea for you and me. When we are under attack because of our circumstances, we will demonstrate a righteous relationship with God if we treasure life as His gracious gift. We should pursue His gift of life and enjoy the relationship He desires to have with us. We demonstrate a righteous character when we embrace rather than reject a relationship with God and pursue the physical and spiritual treasures He has prepared for us.

Will your relationship with God withstand the challenge of circumstances and others? Is it something you have embraced? I trust it is. We have talked about our relationship with God several times, and it is simple to initiate. God, who has given life, desires to have a relationship with us that does not begin or end when our physical lives cease. Eternal life comes through the provision of the cross and the death of Jesus. Sin separates us from God; sin is the stuff we want to do rather than what He wants us to do. We choose to live in rebellion to God. Most of us do not have to think too hard to remember some of those choices. God knew He needed to solve that problem, and His solution was the cross. Jesus died in our place for our sins. He took the punishment we deserve. When we celebrate communion, it reminds us that the shed blood, the broken body, provided forgiveness for our sins. It is not about what we do to earn it but what God has done to provide it. We need to own that our sins put Him there to pay the price. We must receive forgiveness as a gift and thank Him for it.

Some people believe they are saved because they walked an aisle, raised a hand, or repeated a prayer. These illustrate only that salvation is about a new birth (John 3:3), not the behavior of the baby. It is not my intention to diminish any of those actions, but if we do not have a heart transformation that allows God to be God, we are sinners still separated from Him, and our hearts must be reoriented. Our spiritual citizenship must be moved from the kingdom of darkness to the kingdom of Jesus (Col. 1:13).

Like Job, you can know you are not wicked. Job knew that God was the giver of physical and spiritual life, an ever-present gift. Job knew that the wicked reject God but that he had an ongoing relationship with God, who provided for his needs with the treasure of earth. These are how a champion knows he is walking with God.

CHAPTER 14
Job, the Man
Job 29:1–31:40

Job, an amazing man, was confident in his relationship with God. Theoretically, in this chapter we should be looking at his third exchange with Zophar, as Eliphaz and Bildad had had three turns each, and this would be Zophar's third turn. However, he did not speak; he apparently had nothing to say.

In chapters 29 through 31, we have Job's last speech with his friends. In our last chapter, Job defended himself from the accusation of being a wicked man. In this section, he positively addressed who he was, talking about his life story. In the next chapter, we will look at the speech of Elihu. He was frustrated by what he had heard, so he felt the need to set people straight. Following Elihu, we have the moment we have anticipated: God entered the discussion. God would set everyone straight and tell them how it was. However, reading with that expectation will generate serious disappointment. We still have plenty to learn about God.

Before we turn our attention to chapter 29, let us take a few moments to remind ourselves of Job's last exchange. Job, in the midst of chaos, had been dealing with his friends who had attacked his character, thinking he was wicked and had offended God. In reality, this was the outworking of a spiritual challenge between Satan and God. In the last chapter, we reflected on the differences between Job and wicked people. They did not value life as a gift from God or His physical and spiritual provision for them and had rejected Him. Job, an individual of character, valued God and what He had provided. Job understood wonderful truths about God that Bildad did not.

Maybe Zophar's silence illustrated the truth of 1 Peter 2:15: "For such is the will of God that by doing right you may silence the ignorance of foolish men." Job's friends had repeatedly demonstrated their ignorance of God and His ways and had an appalling lack of insight into the spiritual dimension of life for those who gave counsel. Silence must have seemed like the best option.

So who is Job? We have heard what God had to say. We understand what Eliphaz, Bildad, and Zophar had to say. Who Job is will be the focus of this chapter. Who is this person no one is like? Who is this individual who has spoken what was right of God? We are going to consider three characteristics of Job. I encourage you to read chapters 29 through 31. In our discussion, we are going to select various verses to demonstrate three significant characteristics. While they are not unique, they are surprising in the life of Job, who was faithful to what God had expected of him, a champion.

The first characteristic I want us to understand is that Job was a phenomenally compassionate person who showed it in his behavior. He told us in Job 29:12–13, "Because I delivered the poor who cried for help and the orphan who had no helper. The blessing of the one ready to perish came upon me, and I made the widow's heart sing for joy." Job was actively engaged in the lives of the poor, the suffering, and the widows. He helped those who had no one to defend them. This was a male-dominated culture. A woman who did not live in her husband's house had better be living in her father's house. A woman without a male protector could be in serious trouble with nowhere to turn. The culture did not provide government assistance. Because Job understood who God was and what

God desired, he was actively engaged in touching hurting lives. In verse 15 we see another group of people. "I was eyes to the blind and feet to the lame." In verse 17, he said, "I broke the jaws of the wicked and snatched the prey from his teeth." Job was an individual who saw the hurting world around him and was willing to invest his resources, his time, and his reputation to help those in need. There are not many like that today. No wonder he was God's champion! Job knew those he assisted and was affected by touching their lives.

In Job 31:29 and following, he says, "Have I rejoiced at the extension of my enemy or exulted when evil befell him? No, I have not allowed my mouth to sin by asking for his life in a curse." The verses continue to defend his character and compassion. They show that he also invested in his enemies and travelers or foreigners. That might remind us of the story of the Good Samaritan (Luke 10:30–37). Jesus answered the question regarding who was a neighbor, the one in need of our help, and Job lived that story. He supported the lives of foreigners, those to whom he had no obligation. He helped strangers he would probably never see again. He invested in people who had nothing to offer him, those who would be an expense, a drain on his resources. He would not condemn or curse even his enemies.

Job was a living illustration of Jesus' words in the Sermon on the Mount regarding enemies (Matt. 5:43–47). Jesus challenged them to love their enemies, to live better than those who hated them. This was very characteristic of Job's life, as he was a compassionate, caring individual. He demonstrated where he lived the reality of his relationship with God and was as such an example for us to emulate. His compassion translated into real acts of kindness. He behaved like the champion God knew he was.

Let us consider a second characteristic of Job, someone God had singled out. Job championed a right relationship with God, a relationship built on who God was rather than that which God gave or that which Job, a person of character and integrity, did.

It would be good to turn to Job 29, where we find this truth regarding Job's character. Job 29:14, which follows the verses about the widow and orphan, said, "I put on righteousness, and it clothed me; my justice was like a robe and a turban." Job overtly declared his righteous, an ever-present characteristic. He said he wrapped himself in godly behavior visible to everybody. When you put on a coat, everybody can see it, while there are articles of clothing others do not see. Our lives can be the same way; they can have aspects others may not see. They may speak to our character but are not obvious. For Job, however, his righteousness, which wrapped him as his outer garment, was obvious; it was the article of his clothing the world could see.

He continued in chapter 31 in a question format that made declarations. In verses 5 and 6, he said, "If I have walked with falsehood, and my foot has hastened with deceit, let him weigh me with accurate scales, and let God know my integrity." Job made the point he was a truth teller. He did not practice deceit or misrepresentation. If he had, he understood he would not have represented God well.

He said in verses 7 and 8, "If my step has turned from the way, or my heart followed my eyes, or if any spot has stuck to my hands, let me sow and another eat, and let my crops be uprooted." This was an expanded declaration. In verse 1 he said, "I have made a covenant with my eye; how then could I gaze at a virgin." He was speaking of lust. Therefore, in verse 7 when he spoke of his steps and eyes, we know his reference and his intent. He had moral character and did not lust after women. The treatment of women was a cultural problem. We read in the Old Testament how some men conducted themselves with women, but Job was an example of singular character.

At verses 13 and 14 he said, "If I have despised the claims of my male or female slaves when they filed a complaint against me, what then can I do when God arises? And when He calls me to account, what will I answer Him?" He claimed he treated his workers fairly, and verse 15 tells us why. He believed that the same Creator made them both. He did not see himself as better than his workers. He believed he and they had the same standing before God, who had fashioned them and had given them life. Job believed his position was a trust from God, so he had no business using his position as a steward to bully or mistreat others. His record was that of treating his workers fairly. As a master, he was not obligated to do so within his culture, but he was obligated by his relationship with God. Job was an individual of character, as any good champion should be.

In verses 38–40, Job said, "If my land cries out against me, and its furrows weep together; if I have eaten its fruit without money, or have caused its owners to lose their lives, let briars grow instead of wheat, and stink weed instead of barley." This is the picture God used with Cain when he killed his brother (Gen. 4:10). The land is pictured as crying out because of bloodshed, idolatry, or poor treatment of people. Jesus stated that the rocks would cry out if the people did not (Luke 19:40). Job used the imagery of the land because it endures. People come, go, live, and die, but the land remains as a witness, so he called on it to be a witness regarding his business practices, his treatment of others, and the integrity of his dealings. He was ready to give up everything if he had not operated ethically. Job was making statements in a question format. He was a person of integrity and conducted himself with ethical character in business.

Job was a compassionate person who demonstrated it in his relationships. He benefited even his enemies. He operated in righteousness, truth, and morality. He was fair in business; even his treatment of his workers was above reproach. Job was an amazing man. No wonder he was God's champion in this spiritual battle with Satan.

Job was also a man of faith. He did not do what he did because he thought he was going to get something out of it or felt coerced. He lived a blameless, upright life because he was a man of faith who walked with God. He had a relationship with the God of eternity that set standards for those who love God. Let us go back to chapter 29, as Job has intertwined these ideas in his defense. Job was a man of faith and spoke of his friendship with God in Job 29:2–5. They sound like memorable times; Job was reminiscing about better days. He declared his friendship with God; it was a covering over his tent. He declared God was his light when he walked in darkness. He spoke of a rich and meaningful relationship with God, who watched over Job. It was a relationship on which God could stake His reputation and an example to which we could aspire in our pursuit of God.

In his reminiscing, he made other comments about God. Let us consider Job 30:19–20: "He has cast me into the mire, and I have become like dust and ashes. I cried out to You for help, but you did not answer me; I stand up, and You turn your attention against me." In the next couple of verses it becomes obvious that Job was not very happy with God; we addressed this issue in chapter 5 (Job 3:1–26). We asked if it was all right to complain, and I answered with a resounding "Yes! It is alright to complain." These verses sound like an indictment of God. In light of that, let us remember the end of the book. God will declare that Job had spoken what was right about Him (Job 42:7). God's analysis of Job's words was part of how we concluded it must be okay to complain.

God's shoulders are broad enough to take responsibility for the things in our lives. God is not in heaven wringing His hands and worrying about whether you and I are going to upset the order of the universe. He is not concerned about our action or inaction impacting the accomplishment of His will. God is in control of heaven and earth. You may have heard people say they have learned He is God and they are not, and all of us need to arrive at that point in our lives. He is God and we are not. For us to complain to God about what He has overseen does not upset God in the least. Job experienced the same tragedies regardless of how and why they happened. In our lives, we do too. Let us, in our relationships with God, not be concerned about our analysis of what we are experiencing. We made that observation from Hebrews in which God invited us to come boldly into His presence (Heb. 4:16). He did not say we should come only when things are good. It was "to help in times of need." God does not say, "I do not want to hear it." That is not the God of heaven and earth. When we come boldly into His presence, we can come with the frustrations of our hearts. The things Job experienced would cause anybody frustration, so let us not live in pious religiosity and declare Job should not have been bothered by the circumstances of his life. Let us grant him the freedom of his relationship with God.

Job's losses are unimaginable. He even lost the positive encouragement of his wife. A long time before all that would have happened to me, I would have lost Job's positive attitude. After he had lost everything except his health, he said, "The Lord gave and the Lord has taken away. Blessed be the name of the Lord" (Job 1:21). When I lose stuff, I am not happy about it. My first thought is not, "Blessed be the name of the Lord."

As a man of faith, Job cried out to God in good times and bad. He expressed his heart openly to God. He was willing to come into God's presence regardless of the circumstances. Is that not the characteristic of a long-term friendship? Friends share the joys of life as well as its frustrations, and we have to be able to tell our friends when we are ticked and when we rejoice. Job's faith-based friendship with God could endure all.

We discussed Job 31:15 earlier in the chapter. Job addressed the reason for his integrity with his workers. He said that the one who made him also made his workers. Job understood that God was in control and was willing to submit to His care. Proof of that is in Job 31:24–28.

> If I have put my confidence in gold, and called fine gold my trust, if I have gloated because of my wealth was great, and because my hand had secured so much; if I have looked at the sun when it shown or the moon going in splendor, and my heart became secretly enticed, and my hand threw a kiss from my mouth, that

133

too would have been an iniquity calling for judgment, for I would have deny God above.

Job did not rely on his possessions or on idols, alternatives to God just in case. He did not have a plan B. Job was in total dependence and reliance upon God, and that is the hallmark of faith and a true champion.

Job was a man of faith who lived it, a man of compassion who expressed it, a man of character who demonstrated it. As we see Job in this context, we begin to understand the beginning of the process. It makes sense that God said to Satan, "Have you considered my servant Job?" (Job 1:8). He was an amazing individual who had an awesome relationship with God.

How is this working in your life? I trust you are allowing the spirit of God to be at work in you. His friendship will change you. You should be in cooperation with Him, building these characteristics. It is God's desire for us to become more compassionate. He has a goal of higher integrity and greater faith. Let us consider 1 Peter 3:16–17.

> And keep a good conscience so that in the thing
> in which you are slandered, those who revile
> your good behavior in Christ will be put to
> shame. For it is better, if God should will it so,
> that you suffer for doing what is right rather
> than for doing what is wrong.

That is exactly where Job was living. His integrity was in his walk and in his friendship with God. He was suffering in spite of his integrity, his compassion, and his faith, but He silenced his accusers. Peter said it was a lot better to suffer for doing right than to suffer because you deserved it.

I trust you are not motivated to avoid suffering. Jesus tells us that in the world we will experience tribulation (John 16:33) and that the world will hate us (John 15:19). Peter's words seemed to imply that we are going to suffer, but there is a right way and a wrong way to suffer. Peter recognized that suffering can come on either side of the spectrum. We can be doing what is wrong and suffer for it. We can be doing what is absolutely right, nothing wrong in our lives, and we can be suffering. One example is the man born blind (John 9:1–3). The disciples come along and asked Jesus, "Who sinned, this man or his parents?" In unbiblical thinking, there is a correlation between suffering and sin. Jesus said, "The blindness does not have anything to do with him, his parents, or sin. It is about the glory of God." Suffering in our lives has to do with the glory of God. That is the truth of Peter's statement about suffering when we do what is right. We did not do anything to deserve it or justify it. It is just like salvation, a gift from God. This is the experience and reality of life.

I hope we can all look at the undeserved suffering in our lives and see God at work and His glory. Let us continue to become a people who are growing in our compassion, integrity, and faith, champions with a cause.

CHAPTER 15
Wolves in Sheep's Clothing
Job 32:1–37:24

This chapter will look at Elihu, who spoke after Eliphaz, Bildad, and Zophar. They have claimed in one way or another that Job, a wicked person who experienced the judgment of God, had failed. Job responded to each attack with the persistent claim that he was right before God. His losses were not the result of unrighteousness in his life or God's judgment.

Having covered most of the book of Job, we understand there were days when Job would have preferred death. Nevertheless, he does not fall into Satan's trap. In spite of all he has experienced, he does not curse God. When we mentally step away from the book and look at an overview, we see God declared there was no one like Job at the beginning (Job 1:8), and at the end of the book, God said Job had spoken what was right about Him (Job 42:7). It should seem obvious that attributing error to Job, justifying his friends' arguments, and thus concluding that Satan was right and God was wrong about Job is inappropriate and counterproductive to biblical Christianity.

This difference of perspective brings us to Elihu. Human beings have some common flaws in their thinking, and Elihu illustrates one. People tend to think if there is a conflict, the resolution is somewhere in the middle. Have you found that in your own thinking? If there are two individuals, two groups, or two ideologies at odds, truth and reality are somewhere between them. There is a serious flaw in that logic. When God's truths or principles are involved, right is on one side, God's. While it is generally true that victors write history, it does not establish truth. If the Axis Powers of World War II had won, their genocide would still have been wrong. If the USSR had won the Cold War, its wholesale slaughter of millions of people, its denial of God, and its economic system would still be wrong. Whether those we call terrorists win in the end, their hatred, their murder of others through suicide, and their sexual fantasies of virgins as rewards are also wrong. Winning does not make evil commendable even if it makes it legal; might does not make right. Elihu demonstrates humanity's efforts and failures to find truth in the middle. God does not negotiate truth or morality.

We find Elihu's speech starting in Job 32. He is an interesting character to study. Many think he is the redemption of the book of Job. Sanity has prevailed in the silence of conflicted error. He is the defender of God. I do not believe these chapters will support that conclusion. In the light of God's conclusions, Elihu was guilty of the same errant thinking as Eliphaz and friends were. In the text, Elihu did not claim to speak for God. He spoke about God and in support of God but not as a voice for God. He claimed to speak for wisdom; he told Job if he wanted to learn wisdom, just listen (Job 33:33). So as we consider this speech by Elihu, we need a frame of reference. Because the Book of Job is a heavenly conflict, I want us to ask, "When Satan realized he had lost, what was the nature of his last-ditch effort?"

When the final push for our defeat comes, and it will come, will we be ready? Job had experienced the most vicious attacks. His family and wealth were gone, and his wife had suggested he curse God and die (Job 2:9). His friends, who had come to comfort him, condemned him for being a wicked individual and accused him of mistreating the poor, the orphan, and his own servants. In our own experiences, after such an attack we sit back, exhale a sigh of relief, and think, *Praise God! I survived.* At that point, the biggest challenge is just ahead. I believe that is where we are in the story of Job.

The well-spoken, likeable Elihu entered the conversation: "I am young in years and you are old; therefore I was shy and afraid to tell you what I think" (32:6). In verse 11 he said, "I waited for your words, I listened to your reasoning, while you pondered what to say." We see that respectful and thoughtful Elihu had listened and had waited his turn. In verse 15 and 16 he commented on Job's friends. They were dismayed; they no longer answered because words had failed them. "Shall I wait, because they do not speak, because they stop and answer no more?" He had been patient. He had let them speak and had not jumped into the conversation. He was a gentleman of his times, everything he ought to be. I intend to demonstrate that such an evaluation is misguided. He simply knew how to charm the crowd. Have you ever been in a situation of conflict and after you survived the attack, there is someone charming, thoughtful, gracious and well spoken who steps into the situation and cuts your heart out? That is Elihu.

In answer to our question, "What does a last-ditch effort look like?" it will be conducted by people like Elihu. They will be thoughtful, respectful, well liked, and reasonable. They will insert themselves into the situation, charm the crowd, and seek to solicit general respect due to their character. However, this does not tell us their true intentions or motivations. They could be either saint or sleazebag. Over and over, people demonstrate they look on outward appearances (1 Sam. 16:7). They appear nice looking, well spoken, respectful, and well intentioned. Many who write about Job draw that conclusion. However, Elihu shared the values of Eliphaz and friends (see Appendix B).

A second answer to our question is that they will chide the accusers. Look at Job 32:3: "And his anger burned against his three friends because they had found no answer, and yet had condemned Job." They condemned Job and yet had not made one convincing argument to justify their condemnation. He tried to align himself with Job by attacking Job's accusers. Note verse 12: "I even paid close attention to you; indeed, there was no one who refuted Job, not one of you who answered his words." He told Eliphaz, Bildad, and Zophar that they had nothing to say. They were angry with Job; they condemned him but had not made one good point. Verse 14 tells us, "For he has not arranged his words against me, nor will I reply to him with your arguments." Elihu was going to speak, but he was not going to follow the reasoning of his friends. Their logic had been unsuccessful because they had been wrong.

Job, stewing in his troubles, may have thought that someone finally understood him, that someone who realized what was happening was going to support him. This nice guy who had charmed the crowd and chided his accusers was there to help. Get ready; it is going downhill.

Elihu claimed to support and identify with Job. In Job 33:4–7, Elihu said, "The Spirit of God has made me, and the breath of the Almighty gives me life. Refute me if you can; array yourselves before me, take your stand. Behold, I belong to God like you; I too have been formed out of the clay." If we look back at Job's arguments, we find each of these ideas was used first by Job. He on his own behalf had stated that God had made him (Job 10:8), that the breath of God was in him (Job 27:3), and that he had been formed from the earth (Job 10:9). Inversely, he declared the hand of God weighed heavily on him (Job 23:2) and the words of his friends were crushing (Job 19:2). Elihu said that he had paid close attention and that this demonstrated his claim. He said in the next verse his words would not weigh on Job. In Job 33:32, he said, "Then if you have anything to say, answer me; speak, for I desire to justify you." Elihu, this nice guy who was respectful, chided Job's accusers, identified with Job, and then expressed a desire to justify him. He was acting as though he agreed with and supported Job.

Let us not be confused even if Job may have been. Elihu did not support or agree with Job. We have the whole story and know what was about to happen. When Satan wants to grab hold of you and strangle the life out of you where you have felt the heat of conflict and the disapproval of friends, he will send someone into the battle who appears to be a supporter. Beware! Charming the crowd, chiding the accusers, claiming his support, he is about to attack.

As he claimed, Elihu did not attack as Eliphaz, Bildad, and Zophar had. He took the words Job used regarding God and condemned him. We need to remind ourselves about God's observation regarding Job's words. He spoke correctly about God (Job 42:7). If we do not keep that fact clear in our thinking, we may draw the mistaken conclusion that Elihu was defending God. By using Job's words about God to condemn him, Elihu demonstrated he did not understand who God was, just like Job's other three friends. In Job 33:12, Elihu quoted Job's words about God and concluded, "Behold, let me tell you, you are not right in this." He condemned Job for what he had said about God. Elihu was not defending God. We know God declared Job to be right. Elihu was wrong in his analysis, and we are wrong if we defend him and reject God's defense of Job.

Eliphaz and friends were the bad cops and Elihu was the good cop. Elihu was the nice guy who would help Job. But after he charmed the crowd, condemned Job's accusers, and expressed his support, he hammered Job. Elihu told Job that his declarations about God were incorrect. In 34:7–8, he asked, "What man is like Job, who drinks up derision like water, who goes in company with the workers of iniquity, and walks with wicked men?" Elihu condemned Job regarding his relationship with God and his understanding of that relationship. A little later in Job 34:35, Elihu said, "Job speaks without knowledge, and his words are without wisdom. Job ought to be tried to the limit, because he answers like wicked men. For he adds rebellion to his sin; he claps his hands among us, and multiplies his words against God." That does not sound as though he is on the same page with God regarding Job's words. Elihu, who thought Job had gotten what he had deserved and maybe should have gotten more, was not the good cop. Let us move on to Job 35:13 and 16: "Surely God will not listen to an empty cry, nor will the Almighty regard it. So Job opens his mouth emptily; he multiplies words without knowledge." Elihu accused Job of wickedness, which God ultimately did not support.

As we have skimmed through Elihu's speech, there seems to be no difference between his conclusions and those of Eliphaz, Bildad, and Zophar, who had condemned Job of wickedness and misrepresenting God. The difference was that Elihu used Job's words, while Eliphaz, Bildad, and Zophar fabricated condemnation of Job's actions and attitudes based on their assumptions. Elihu condemned Job's view of God with the arguments used in his defense. Because Elihu did not know God as Job did, he believed Job was wrong, but his condemnation was built on his assumptions regarding God, just like the other three accusers.

Elihu must have been an early proponent of the political concept of triangulation. When two groups are at odds with one another, you support and challenge both while offering a middle path toward progress or resolution. The problem for Elihu rested in his assumptions. God is truth. Job spoke what was right about God. There was not a correct middle path somewhere else. When we make assumptions about how we serve God, how we bless Him, and how others are to do the same, we fall into the historic problem of self-righteousness. We accept the validity of performance-based religion and cause-and-effect spirituality. While this is common in the world we have addressed previously, Elihu held these values to be true. They are, however, unbiblical and counterproductive to true spirituality.

We learn in Scripture as captured by the Westminster Confession that the chief end of man is to glorify God. When we deviate from that goal, we find ourselves in trouble. We will be making assumptions just like Job's friends. Job's detractors assumed the chief end of man was to demonstrate the justice of God. Because God is righteous and just, Job must be wicked. If you do what is right, you are blessed. If you do what is wrong, you are condemned. Because of this assumption and the fact that Job was apparently being judged, the logical conclusion was that Job was wicked and had done wrong. They did not have as a part of their thinking that something else might have been going on to the glory of God.

At the end of the book, the fundamental issue is God's glory. In the heavenly conflict that initiates the story, it is not about Job; it is about God's glory. Satan attacked God. Job was nothing more than the source of Satan's attack. Satan believed Job would condemn God. Job and his friends were only the players in this spiritual conflict. We tend to treat them as the stars when they had only bit parts. Everything recorded was based on the conflict between God and Satan, and God's glory was revealed in what happened. If any of Job's friends had accepted the idea that there was something more significant happening than the obvious experiences of life, they might have drawn different conclusions. However, if we have the view that God is a righteous judge who blesses the good and punishes the bad, we are living in the same assumptions as Job's accusers. Elihu is no exception. Because he elevated God to being strictly a righteous judge, Job deserved his troubles and maybe worse. He concluded that Job had not measured up. Whether we focus on God as judge or God's righteousness, we, like Job's friends, will draw the same incorrect conclusions. God is more than a righteous judge. As noted previously, Jesus' disciples had the same problem with the man born blind.

Jesus experienced the reality of wrong assumptions about God. He walked this earth as the Son of God. He stepped into time to go to the cross and die for our sins. His contemporaries did not understand why He was there. They struggled to understand His spiritual mission because of their assumptions about God and how He would enter into time. The religious leaders did not understand, and even His disciples did not really grasp what was happening because they had a different perspective on God's work on earth. After the resurrection, the disciples who had been with Jesus and had seen the miracles, who had been depressed by the crucifixion and then elated by the resurrection, wanted to know if Jesus was going to set up His kingdom. They still did not understand who God was and what He was doing in the world. They missed God's fundamental relational nature and His desires. Errant views take us down wrong paths to wrong conclusions.

Cause-and-effect spirituality is as much a part of the spiritual assumptions of humanity today as it was in Job's time. It is common both outside and inside the church. This assumption exposes a misguided characteristic of our human nature. If we were to travel to an animist culture that believed in tree spirits, river spirits, spirits of the ancestors, and spirits in control of all aspects of life, we would probably be surprised by their view of life and might even ask why. They are trying to appease the spirits. If they succeed, they will be blessed; if they fail, they will suffer harm. It is easy to see their cause-and-effect view of spirituality, but it is a lot harder to understand this view of spirituality in our own thinking and Christian community.

When I was a Christian school administrator, one family had a picture of a luxury car they wanted. They were convinced that as soon as they got their act together, God would bless them with the car, the desire of their hearts (Ps. 37:4). Sadly, many Christians live in the same incorrect notion of God as the animists in other parts of the world. Whether we are trying to be blessed by pleasing the spirits or by pleasing God, it is the same errant understanding of God. Whether we are trying to avoid negative consequences by pleasing the spirits or by pleasing God, it is a wrong view of spirituality. It has been and will always be wrong. That is not who God is, nor is it the basis of biblical faith. It is not the basis of our spirituality or the basis of our relationship with God. If we have to be good enough for God's acceptance, it will never happen. Amazingly and inexplicably, God has loved us and has made provision for us. He has called us to himself and embraced us in His love. He has forgiven our sins through the shed blood of Jesus Christ. What a wonderful provision from a God who loves us and wants a relationship with us!

Job could not have articulated these truths, but he knew his Redeemer lived, he knew he was a friend of God, and he knew he walked with God, who loved him and provided for him. He also knew the experiences of life did not affect or reflect his relationship with God, which was secure, and he knew he would see God in the resurrection. He knew that he was a steward of what God entrusted to his care and that God could give and could take away. These things he could tell his friends. He did not buy into the idea that he had been blessed because he had been good and that he was suffering because he had been bad. He refused to accept the cause-and-effect spirituality of his friends; he believed in a relational God who created and loved him.

If we accept the premise of Job's friends, there are many in history who will not fit the model of such thinking. Fox's *Book of Martyrs* is a lengthy list of those who served and loved Jesus but paid for their spiritual behavior with their lives. The unimaginable horrors they experienced were hardly the reward or blessing for living lives pleasing to God. *Tortured for Christ,* by Richard Wormbrandt, and *I Was a Slave in Russia,* by John S. Noble, are other books that describe the horrendous treatment of God's people. God's people, living lives pleasing to Him, have not always experienced the blessings and joys of life. If we accept the rational of Elihu, they all deserved it. They failed a righteous God and may have deserved worse than they experienced.

We need to live in God's mercy and friendship. We may experience difficulty, loss, and heartache, we may move from a place of blessing to a place of suffering, persecution, and possible death, but that will have nothing to do with the unbiblical notion we have been bad. God is always good to us in the experiences of blessing and the experiences of frustration and suffering. He is good to us because His love is not limited by our choices. It does not depend on our good behavior. God loves us intensely and so much that He was willing to experience suffering and death in our place. Elihu missed the true nature of God's grace and mercy, and his thinking will lead us in the wrong direction.

When conflict calms down, beware of wolves in sheep's clothing. They come charming the crowd and condemning your accusers. They will appear to take your side. Their vicious attack is about to be unleashed. However, God's grace is adequate to be victorious.

Chapter 16

Thus Saith the Lord

Job 38:1–41:34

In Job chapters 38 through 41, God stepped onto the scene and did what? It is an interesting dilemma. The common wisdom says that God reproved Job, took him to task, chided him on his poor behavior, and condemned him. This far into the book, I am going to wonder about drawing that conclusion because it does not seem to comport with the relationship between God and Job. God had told Satan, "There is no one like him" (Job 1:8), and throughout the book Job spoke what was right about God (Job 42:7). There is nothing in these four chapters that should have changed God's assessment at the beginning or the end of the book. If this is a condemnation of Job, God has conceded Satan was right. I do not believe that happened. However, let us not jump to the conclusion that godly men are perfect men. The next chapter will address Job's response.

This is a book about God, whose actions are read about here and throughout Scripture. Who is the God of the Bible? Does He behave as an aloof judge without recourse? In Genesis 1–3, we see God as Creator of all that exists, including man, whom God said was very good. He desired a relationship with Adam and Eve. We learn there are consequences for man's poor behavior. Nevertheless, we do not see God in an indifferent judicial role condemning Adam and Eve for eating the fruit. We have grace, a promise of a savior. We do not see God in an exacting judicial role regarding David's adultery and murder. We have grace, Solomon in the line of Messiah. We do not see God in an intolerant judicial role with the nation of Israel. He warned Israel for decades. We have grace; the nation returned to the land God promised to Abraham. We do not see heaven rolled back and God pronouncing unequivocal judgment. We do not see God in the fullness of His judicial role until we get to Revelation; no grace, no recourse.

At the end of time, after this world has served its purpose and God says enough is enough, we will see God in His full judicial capacity. Humanity will be faced with eternal judgment or reward. In the meantime, Jesus said He had come "to seek and save the lost" (Luke 19:10). He said He did not come to judge the world but to save it (John 12:47). We see a compassionate God throughout Scripture, drawing humanity to Himself in His compassion, love, and desire for fellowship. It is His expressed desire to see all men saved (1 Tim. 2:4).That is the picture we have of God from the beginning to the end of Scripture, and it should be His character in the book of Job.

To anticipate a judicial pronouncement against Job seems a bit out of character if this is a book about God. If this book were about Job, maybe he needed to be chastised. "A blameless and upright man" (Job 1:8) is not necessarily a perfect man. David certainly deserved it. At least a few significant sins were a part of his life experience. Moses was not a shining star of godly character, but God spoke with him "face to face" (Ex. 33:11) and gave the Ten Commandments twice. There are several of questionable moral character in the linage of Jesus. Peter or the murderous Saul might come to mind. Even when we see legitimate opportunity for God to step in and condemn people, we do not see Him functioning as judge. That does not mean that they got away with anything. Psalm 51 is David's repentance. He was broken, one who had failed God. This "man after God's own heart" (1 Sam. 13:14) had failed to pursue God perfectly and had failed in his relationship with the God who loved him. David responded to God's love and grace just as Paul had. God's grace, forgiveness, and love constrained, motivated, and drove him to do what he did (Cor. 5:14). Micah tells us the Lord's expectations: "To do justice, to love kindness, and to walk humbly with your God" (Mic. 6:8).

So what picture of God do we have? How would God present Himself? I suggest we have a picture of a compassionate God. His servant, unlike any other, who spoke what was right, was hurting. God stepped onto the stage of life to comfort a disquieted heart. Job was upset and troubled and may have been angry. I think the appropriate question to ask regarding these chapters is, "How does God comfort a disquieted heart?" How does God comfort us in a situation when we are upset? The circumstances have been against us. Our friends have not been supportive. Intended comforters have been confrontational. We feel abandoned and are expressing our frustrations to God. How does God step into that situation? Should we expect His criticism? We have been there at one level or another; life can be difficult.

Sadly, most people live with the perception that others really do not care and God exists to condemn us for our failures. They see God as one who will bless good behavior and condemn bad behavior. They have a performance-based view of God, but this is not the God of the Bible. God is compassionate and cares about people. When we are in Job's place of frustration, pain, and confusion, we need comfort, encouragement, and support. God will bring peace to our troubled hearts. Our past experiences may have taught us that hope or encouragement comes from a change in perspective more than a change in circumstance. God wants to bring us a change in perspective. In these chapters, we will see four truths God used to change or reorient the perspective of Job. In the next chapter, we will see Job's response to God's grace.

The first thing God did was in Job 38:4. It established the issue with a simple question, "Where were you when I laid the foundation of the earth?" Over the next seven verses, God asked Job a series of questions. We tend to interpret Job in our Western, occidental, linear thinking rather than in the context of its Eastern, cyclical thinking. You may be familiar with the early Greeks and the peripatetic method of teaching. They walked around and asked questions. That was based more in Eastern, Middle Eastern, thinking. Thus God asked instructive questions of Job. Verse 2 asked, "Who is this that darkens counsel?" At face value in our Western thinking, it sounds as though God was reproving Job. Yet if we think in a more Eastern approach, it was just a question. Job had been making claims, asking questions, and demanding an audience with God. In context, God was asking about the person who wanted to speak with Him. If God was going to answer Job's questions, there were certain things needed to establish a frame of reference before He could give an understandable answer. God's questions were seeking common ground. Job's perspective needed to change, and our perspective may need to change also.

God brings us to a place of change. We have been in the place of asking the why questions, frustrated by events. God came along and reminded us He had made it all. He understood why planets stay in orbit, why comets do not crash into the sun. He understood why there seems to be an expanding universe. God said if you do not understand how the earth spins in the middle of nothingness, we are going to have a problem communicating. Do you understand why the ocean stops at the shore? We have been there. God reminded us He was God and had created it all. In Genesis 1:1 is the declaration, "In the beginning God created the heavens and the earth." John 1:3 tells us all things exist because of Him. God is the Creator, and as such He has insight and understanding that goes beyond anything our finite understanding can grasp. There are answers we would not understand even if He gave them. We do not have enough information to make sense of what we would be told.

Let us consider a real-life example. Most parents do not look forward with excited anticipation to the "Where do babies come from?" question. Children usually ask it somewhere between the ages of two and four, but they have no ability to understand the answer and are not ready for the "birds and bees" discussion. They just need a simple answer. A child may ask, "How do planes fly?" They are not ready for a lesson in aerodynamics. Many questions, like college classes, have prerequisites. They require a certain level of knowledge to enable an understanding of the answers. God helped Job grasp that he did not have the requisite knowledge for an answer. Often when we are frustrated, we need to realize we do not have a clue. In these verses, God helped Job understand he was clueless. Even if God gave him an answer, he would not understand. God gives simple answers, sometimes through questions, because that is what we can handle. God, who created the world, spent most of chapter 38 dealing with His creative actions. These are accomplishments Job did not have the capacity to understand.

At Job 38:39, we see God move from His responsibility as Creator to maintainer. "Can you hunt the prey for the lion, or satisfy the appetite of the young lions, when they crouch in their dens and lie in wait in their lairs?" Job 39:5–6 asked, "Who sent out the wild donkey free? And loosed the bonds of the swift donkey, to whom I gave the wilderness for a home, and the salt land for his dwelling place?" Verse 13 started a discussion of the ostrich. Verse 19 took up wild horses. God affirmed He created the world and kept it running.

God knows how to maintain order and provide for its needs. God knows how to provide for the birds of the air, for the lions in the field, and for the goats on the mountains. God understands life and the way it operates in all its complexities. God declared He maintains all that is happening. Hebrews 1:3 says that God "upholds all things by the word of his power." To this day, the world continues to spin; clocks can be set to twenty-four hours; and our calendars advance at 365 1/4 days a year. God maintains the order of the universe. The tide ebbs and flows, the sun rises and sets, the seasons cycle because God is in control. He is not an absentee landlord.

As for us, we can find comfort and encouragement in His control. Chaos and uncertainty create fear. I have often said, "The world has not spun out of control. God is not wringing His hands, wondering, 'What am I going to do now?'" We can find peace in the fact that God runs the world. Jesus told us in Matthew 10:29 that a sparrow does not fall to the ground without God knowing it. God is intimately acquainted with the circumstances and experiences of life, and nothing catches Him by surprise. He was involved with our prenatal formation (Ps. 139:13–16). When we find ourselves crying out to God, to our friends, or just empty space because it feels good to complain, God is there. He wants to remind us that He is the Creator and that nothing escapes His attention. He maintains the world and provides for its needs. We can find comfort in Him, His power, and His authority.

God does not want us to lose sight of the fact that He is the judge. Ignoring His position would not bring comfort, but knowing the judge should. God brings comfort in His position as judge in chapter 40. Verse 8 says, "Will you really annul my judgment? Will you condemn Me that you may be justified." He continues through verse 14 to challenge Job's abilities to intervene as judge. God said He was the judge and could act. He declared He knew how to address the issues of life. The wicked were not going to get away with anything; the proud were not going to stand in their arrogance; He was God, and He was the judge. He knew how to deal with every circumstance of life. He was helping Job understand the implications of his frustration.

When we make declarations about not liking the way things are or that we would have done it differently, we are making an evaluation of God's ability to operate His universe appropriately. We need to understand what we are doing. God helped Job with perspective. In the same way, He compassionately helps us understand He will take care of circumstances in His time, not ours. We may prefer our way and our timing, but God knows better.

Paul addressed a very specific application of this truth in Romans 12:19. He told us to "leave room for the wrath of God." Paul understood in those situations that seem to deserve judgment, God may choose not to exercise His judicial authority in this life or in our time. It is not our job to exercise God's authority. We need to leave room for God to act. I understand we would rather do it ourselves. However, that shares common ground with the same expression by a two-year old.

In the movie *Bruce Almighty*, Bruce is allowed to be God. He does not do a very good job of answering prayers. He just says yes and creates chaos in the world. It is not our job to take care of God's tasks if for no other reason than we would not do them very well. God will take care of everything and is perfectly capable of doing so. Job needed to be reminded of—and we need to understand—God's competence. When I am frustrated and angered by what God is allowing in my life and I am not enjoying a warm, fuzzy experience, I am making judgments about God. They may be about His competence, ability, compassion, or some other challenge to God's acting in my best interest. We need to allow God to be God. When we are comfortable with Him being God, being judge, we are at peace.

We asked previously, "Is it alright to complain?" The answer then is the answer now, yes. God has invited us to come boldly into his presence with the good and the bad. We may bring the things that excite us as well as those that frustrate us. When we come into His presence, He does not interrupt and ask only for the good stuff. Sometimes we think, or at least we behave, as though the only thing God wants is our laundry list of prayer requests. "Oh God, by the way, I need this, this, and this. So-and-so needs this. We have this problem over here. God, take care of all that stuff and bless all the missionaries. Amen." God is not afraid of us coming into his presence and saying, "I do not like this. I am frustrated by what You are allowing in my life. I am not happy about it." God's universe is not going to be shattered. However, we need to understand that such an expression is a challenge of His right to be God. Our perspectives probably need to change. Accordingly, God let Job know who was God and who would take care of it.

God created the world. God maintains the world. God is the judge and will judge appropriately. That leaves us one more concept in God's comforting of Job. This last section of verses addresses all kinds of fascinating things (Job 40:15–41:34). God talked about Behemoth and Leviathan. When you read these verses, you have wondered, "What was on God's mind?" There are multiple suggestions. Some equate them with elephants or hippopotami, while others suggest crocodiles or alligators. These are interesting, but none seems to fit the phrasing of the passage well. Some believe God was talking about dinosaurs, real fire-breathing dragons, and they make a pretty good case, but I do not think any of those options gets to the point that God was making with Job. As I pondered this last section of verses for an answer to the question, "How does God show compassion to a discomforted heart?" it seemed God wanted to remind Job He was the master of the unconquerable and the unexplainable, of all we cannot grasp.

God was able; God knew. He understood who or what Leviathan and Behemoth were and how they operated in the world. He was not bothered by the things Job did not understand because He was able to overcome them. God understood the spears and shields between the plates. God said He could draw them out and deal with them. God knew how to be victorious in the circumstance of Job's life. He could handle the things Job could not explain, understand, or master.

It is important for us to remember that God is in control. You have been frustrated with life, maybe often. If you have not, you will. It goes with the nature of humanity, our life experiences. There are times when we want to ask why. We find ourselves in situations we cannot explain and about which we are not happy. We are being challenged by our friends. When the circumstances of our lives are overwhelming, we wonder, *Where's God?* We need a change in perspective.

God wants to step into those situations, as he did with Job, and bring comfort. He does that by reminding us He created everything and is capable of maintaining it. He declares He will adjudicate all the events of life. Last, He affirms He has answers to all bewildering questions and unexplainable mysteries, all that is without clarity in life. God will bring comfort to our hearts when we rest in His understanding.

It is amazing how consistent this is with what Paul told us in Romans chapter 12. God is at work in our lives. God is in the business of conforming us to the image of Christ. Romans 12:1–2 say,

> Therefore, I urge you, brethren, by the mercies of God, to present your bodies a living and holy sacrifice, acceptable to God, which is your spiritual service of worship. And do not be conformed to this world, but be transformed by the renewing of your mind, so that you may prove what the will of God is, that which is good and acceptable and perfect.

Job needed a mind transformation because he had become absorbed in his own perceptions. He was struggling with the circumstances that consumed him. He needed to be brought out of his frustration and see life from God's perspective. As we see the big picture, God's picture, we become transformed into the image of Christ.

Job needed and we need to understand that God created the world and that He is maintaining His creation and will not allow "them" to get away with anything. God will deal with them in His timing, not ours. Job needed—and we need—to understand that God comprehends the mysteries of life and is able to conquer the unconquerable. As we submit to Him, presenting our bodies as living sacrifices, we will find a God of compassion and comfort that brings peace to our disquieted hearts. He will do for us what He did for Job. God's champions are willing to learn new skills and perspectives.

CHAPTER 17

Job's Reply

Job 40:3–5 and 42:1–6

In the last chapter, we asked an interesting, important question about God. We discussed chapters 38 through 41, in which God spoke with Job. We considered if God was correcting an errant Job who needed to get his act together, as his friends had claimed. That would not be the Job at the beginning about whom God said to Satan, "There is no one like him on earth" (Job 1:8). It does not sound like the Job who had represented God in chapter 42, in which He told Eliphaz that he and his friends were in trouble because they had not spoken what was right about God as Job had (Job 42:7). It is my opinion that we have a problem if Job was a wayward individual God corrected and then turned around and said that Job had spoken what was right about Him. God selected Job to represent Him in this epic battle with Satan over the nature of the relationship between God and men. God's position was that it was about the relationship He had with Job. Satan's position was that it was about what God would do for Job or what Job would get out of it. Let us assume God knew what He was saying.

In this exchange between God and Job, which we started in the last chapter, Job did not have much to say, which would be the case for all of us if God made an appearance in our lives.

In this chapter we will discuss Job's responses. Before we deal with Job, let us reconsider God's comments to him. Situations in our lives will push us to ask why they have happened, and we will struggle through the emotion of what is happening and the lack of support from friends and people we thought would be there for us. Our hearts will have that churning discontent. God stepped into Job's situation and spoke, so we asked, "How does God comfort a disquieted heart?" We saw that God made it clear He had created and maintains the world. The third thing God shared with Job was an affirmation that He was the judge, the guy at the end of the day who was going to deal with the issues of life. God assures the discontent heart He is the judge. The last characteristic was that God is the master of the unexplainable and the unconquerable. God knows all things we do not understand. When our hearts are disquieted or disturbed, God will use these truths to comfort and bring us peace.

Job first responded in the middle of God's comments and questions. In Job 40:4–5, he spoke. "Behold, I am insignificant; what can I reply to You? I lay my hand on my mouth. Once I've spoken, then I will not answer; even twice and I will add nothing more." If God brought comfort to Job's heart, the reasonable follow-up question is, "How do we respond to God's comfort?" How did God's champion respond? Is that typical for us? Is that the way we should respond to God's comfort? As the author of a book about God, I need to capture God's heart and not mislead God's people and take them down a road contrary to the health of the body of Christ. The issues of Job, the issues of these two chapters, lay a foundation for our relationship with God.

Let us look at Psalm 34:15–16: "The eyes of the Lord are toward the righteous and His ears are open to their cry. The face of the Lord is against evildoers to cut off the memory of them from the earth." These verses lay the groundwork for God's interaction with Job and his response. If Job was a troublemaker God needed to correct instead of a blameless and upright man (Job 1:8) who spoke what was right about God (Job

42:7), there is an incongruity with these two verses in Psalms. The memory of Job should have been cut off from the earth. However, we have a book of the Bible that celebrates how he championed the character of God in the face of devastating trials. Additionally, God should not have granted his petition for an audience with Him as the cry of his heart. These verses tell us that God's ears are open to the righteous. He cuts off the memory of the evildoer. Job is either a righteous individual God came to comfort in response to the cry of his heart, or the psalmist had no clue of how God operated in the world. God's ears were obviously open to Job's cry.

Let us consider Job's responses to a God of comfort. As you read the verses of Job's response about his insignificance, wondering what he could say, and laying his hand over his mouth, did that remind you of another story in the Scripture? It reminded me of Abraham, the friend of God (Is. 41:8). God showed up with the goal of destroying the city of Sodom. After he sent angels to destroy Sodom, He decided He would not hide what He was going to do from Abraham (Gen. 18:17). In the verses that follow, Abraham debated with God, challenging Him to change His decision to destroy Sodom if there were fifty righteous people there. God agreed that if fifty righteous were there, He would not destroy Sodom. Abraham asked about being five short of that number. Would God destroy Sodom if there were forty-five righteous? God agreed He would not. Abraham kept pushing the number down, to forty, thirty, twenty, and finally ten. Abraham said, "I have ventured to speak" (Gen 18:31), and later, "I shall speak only this once" (Gen. 18:32). When Job said, "Once I have spoken ... even twice, and I will add nothing more" (Job 40:5), it reminded me of this story of God's exchange Abraham.

We do not think that way because our minds are in a very different place. It is easy to make assumptions about attitudes and actions that do not conform to our expectations. Job, as best we can tell, would have lived in the culture of the patriarchs. This approach to negotiating and interacting, even with God, was not a declaration by Job that he had been wrong. He was not saying he did not have his act together but now understood his mistakes. It is too easy to read the following verse and conclude Job was wrong: "Will the faultfinder contend with the Almighty? Let him who reproves God answer it" (Job 40:2). If, as God declared in a couple of chapters, Job spoke what is right about Him (Job 42:7), it is not reasonable to believe Job had been finding fault with God. If Job had been accusing and blaming God, His later statement would have been a lie, a misrepresentation of God.

If we are going to answer the question, "How should we respond to God's comfort?" the first concern is perspective. God is our friend, and Job responded to a friend. He did not demonstrate fear or anxiety. Job responded exactly as Abraham had. Job was not blown away or bewildered, wondering what had happened.

John 15:15 is a part of Jesus' Upper Room discussion with His disciples. It was the place of the Last Supper and His sharing of the broken bread and cup. He knew He was headed to the garden, a trial, and the cross. Jesus said to His disciples, "No longer do I call you slaves, for the slave does not know what his master is doing; but I have called you friends, for all things that I have heard from my Father I have made known to you." God calls us friends; that is why He has given us the Spirit. He will guide and direct us. It is no longer we who live but Christ lives in us (Gal. 2:20). It is why he has given us His Word. We are his friends. When God steps onto the scene of our disquieted hearts, we need that perspective that He is our friend and respond accordingly. Job understood God, his friend, was the Creator of life and the one with whom he had a relationship.

Our second answer to the question is in chapter 42. After God spoke, there was the brief reply we just considered, and then God finished what He had to say. Job replied again in chapter 42 after God had finished. Job spoke in chapter 42:2, "I know that you can do all things, and that no purpose of Yours can be thwarted." Built upon his friendship with God, Job affirmed that the one speaking was the God he knew. Job knew

God could do all things and was in control. Job confirmed what he had previously declared. Job was not confused about God's character or statements.

From chapter 6 through 29 is a long list of concepts Job understood about God. In Job 6:24, Job understood it was God who taught those who err. In Job 6:10, he was unwilling to deny or violate God's words. In Job 7:17–18, God was concerned about man. In verse 21 of the same chapter, God was the one who took away iniquity. In Job 9:2, 3 and 14, God did not accept the self-justified. In the same chapter, verses 7 through 10, God was the one who created all things, which God affirmed in His speech. Later in the same chapter, verses 32 and 33, Job knew he needed a mediator with God.

He needed a mediator, an umpire, one who could place hands on both of them so they could have this debate. He understood that without a mediator he could not have resolution with God. In Job 10:12 and 12:9–10, God was the one who had given life as a gift. In Job 13:15–16, God was the one in whom Job hoped. It was His presence into which he could enter. In Job 14:14–17, God was the one who was going to resurrect his body. Job declared he was going to be resurrected and would see God in his flesh with his own eyes. He was anticipating the resurrection, and God was the source of the resurrection. In Job 19:25, God was the one who was his Redeemer. Job stated that He was his Redeemer. In Job 21:22, God was the one who would judge all men. God knew all things. In Job 23:11–14, God was the one Job was following and the anchor of his faith. In the same chapter, verse 15, Job declared his fear of the Lord and his respect because of who He was. In Job 27:3–4, Job unequivocally stated he would not condemn God. Certainly, by chapter 27 he had every reason to blame God from his earthly perspective. When his wife suggested he curse God and die in chapter 2, he said that was foolish talk, and it does not appear he changed his perspective. He would not condemn God, which was what Satan said he would do (Job 1:11). In Job 29:2–4, Job affirmed God was his friend. This was Job's understanding of God that came from his relationship with

161

the Creator of the universe and is the reason God chose him as his champion in this battle with Satan. Job responded that the one who spoke was the God he knew. When God showed up to comfort Job, he was His friend. God claimed that there was no one like Job and that he spoke what was right of Him. God supported His champion.

The next few verses in chapter 42 give us Job's third response. In verses 3 through 5, he continued his conversation with God. He questioned his understanding and wanted to be taught. He was impressed with meeting God. Sometimes, our relationships with people take on completely new dimensions. In reality, we had no idea and sometimes violate the appropriate boundaries, which can cause conflict between friends. Sometimes it is because there are aspects of their lives we do not understand. In our text, Job said that he had heard with his ears and now he saw with his eyes that God was awesome, more than he knew. He was even more than the amazing list we delineated in the previous point. Job said God was beyond his wildest imagination, more than he could grasp. He had seen, and it demonstrated God was awesome. A couple of verses in 1 Corinthians are helpful; 1 Corinthians 2:9 says,

> But just as it is written, "Things which eye has not seen and ear has not heard, and which have not entered the heart of man, all that God has prepared for those who love Him." For to us God revealed them through the Spirit; for the Spirit searches all things, even the depths of God.

God is beyond our imagination. Sadly, too many try to confine Him by their intellects. The section of the verse quoted is in Isaiah 64:3–4.

> When You did awesome things which we did not expect, You came down, the mountains quaked at Your presence. For from days of old

> they have not heard or perceived by ear, nor has
> the eye seen a God besides You, Who acts on
> behalf of the one who waits for Him.

In this passage, Isaiah was talking about the awesomeness of God and His investment in the lives of people. This text is a specific reference to Israel and what God had done. God had brought Israel out of Egypt. The people of that generation died in the desert, wandering for forty years. They had a hard time wrapping their minds around the unbelievable things God had done and wanted to do. They had seen the plagues in Egypt. They had gone through the Red Sea, had drunk water from the rock, had eaten manna, and had received the Ten Commandments. But when they came to the Promised Land, there were giants in the land. At the border, they did not respond to the awesomeness of God. Isaiah reminded them of their past. God was beyond their wildest imagination. God was capable of dealing with the needs and issues of life. God was an awesome God. Isaiah began with what they had heard and seen. Job addressed what he had heard and seen. God was awesome.

Job responded with the fact that God was his friend. He interacted with the God he knew. He added that He was the God beyond what he knew. The last answer to the question about responding to God's comfort is in verse 6: "Therefore I retract, and I repent in dust and ashes." Job, a righteous man, God's champion, knew when to withdraw. He realized his request was unreasonable. Job had insisted that God come down and deal with his situation. Job did not understand or like it. In God's comforting of Job, he realized he had overstepped the appropriate boundaries of their relationship.

When God moves to quiet our discomforted hearts, when we are frustrated and explaining to God how He should have handled the situation and did not, we eventually come to the place where we realize God is God. When I come to the realization that God is God, I repent of my foolishness and my unreasonable requests and expectations. While God still loves me and invites me to come, I have exceeded reasonable expectations. I will understand my error in thinking God should have done something different from what He did. I will acknowledge the mistake of thinking my way was better. We human beings make too much of this kind of failure. I do not hesitate to call it sin, and I do not want to minimize it. By the same measure, I do not want to blow it out of proportion. Have we not experienced this on a human plane? When comfort is being provided to those who are struggling, they often admit they had overreacted or had been unreasonable.

The Last Supper will illustrate this point. Jesus washed the disciples' feet. Jesus interacted with them and told Peter he was going to deny Him three times, but Peter insisted he would never deny Jesus. He suggested all the rest of them might, but he would die for Him. Did Jesus say, "Okay, you're on your own"? Jesus, in his love for Peter, stood on the beach after the resurrection and restored Peter. Peter's failure did not make him useless or move Him out of the presence or plan of God. It did not move him away from what God was doing or intending. Considering Peter's life apart from his denial in the garden and repentance on the beach, he was not ready to preach Pentecost Sunday. Failure and learning are characteristic of true champions. Prior to these events, Peter was not ready, but God was at work. Peter had been a quivering mess fifty days earlier, but God was still preparing a champion.

We frequently strap on phenomenal burdens of guilt about our poor decisions and actions. I do not want to minimize sin, but it is not the end of the world; it may be part of God's process to transform our lives. We have not become worthless in God's eyes. We are not of less value due to our failures, nor are we of more value because of our successes. God is at work in our lives. He knows who we are in all our fallen humanity. As we grasp who we are, we begin to understand the person God loved and for whom Jesus died. That is captured in 1 John 1:9: "If we confess our sins." We come to the place where we agree with God regarding our condition. That is what Job did; He came to grips with who God really was.

God was not surprised by Job's attitudes, behaviors, or demands. He was Job's friend and knew what had been happening. God did not change His opinion about Job. There was no one like him. He was His champion, a righteous individual who spoke what was right about God. The battle was engaged at the beginning of the book between God and Satan, and Job's life was the battleground. If Job had been a failure in his representation of a relational God, Satan would have won the conflict. However, God won! Job had done what was right. He had spoken what was right about God. He did not need to be perfect to be a champion. A righteous, blameless person is not necessarily a perfect person. Job recognized his incomplete grasp of who God was and the foolishness that caused his inappropriate behavior. As God's champion, he repented. That is what we need to do; repentance brings comfort. As we grow in our relationship with God, we will grow in our understanding of who He is. It will make us aware of new areas in our lives that do not measure up to God's expectations. The proper response is to repent. We should retract and allow Him to teach us. Our failure has not caused God to change His mind. We are heirs (Rom. 8:17). We are his royal priests (1 Pet. 2:9). We are seated with Him (Eph. 2:6). We are chosen and beloved (Col. 3:12). God knows how to walk with us through the experiences of life and fashion us into His prized possessions.

When God comes to comfort, let us respond well. He is a friend we should welcome. He is the God with whom we have built a relationship. He is an awesome, amazing God beyond our capacities to grasp. As we grow in understanding of Him, we will repent. We should not run from His grace but be champions! Our performance is not His measure of love (Rom 5:8).

CHAPTER 18

In Conclusion

Job 42:7–17

It has been an interesting journey through the book of Job. As we look back, we remember Job was in Abraham's time period. We declared at the beginning that this was a book about God, not about Job or suffering. Too often we get caught up in the circumstances of the story and miss the larger picture. As we have journeyed through Job, we have consistently looked at the character and nature of God. In the last chapter, we summarized our champion's understanding of the God he knew. God will be our focus in the last eleven verses of Job as well.

A couple of chapters ago, after everyone had spoken, God stepped onto the scene to speak. We considered God's message to Job. Many have thought God reproved Job for his poor attitude. From a different perspective, I declared that God came to speak comfort to the heart of Job just as He will to our hearts. As we deal with the struggles of life, God often does not bring answers, but He always brings comfort, which we need through the difficulties we face.

In the last chapter, we looked at Job's response to God and noted that Job had responded as a friend and had expressed that this was the God he knew, the God he had represented. He told

Eliphaz, Bildad, Zophar, and anyone who would listen about His friend God. Third, he declared that God was awesome, great, and beyond anything he had previously known. Job had heard with his ears but then had seen with his eyes. What he saw and then knew far exceeded his experiences. Last, because of this new reality, Job had realized he had stepped over the boundary of their friendship, which caused him to repent. This is exactly what we need to do. Whether it is with God or friends, when we cross proper boundaries of our relationship, repentance is the appropriate response of true champions. It was the response of David in Psalm 51.

At the beginning of the book, God said Job was upright and righteous (Job 1:8), and nothing in the book countermands God's analysis. At the end of the book, in this section, God declared that Job had spoken what was right about Him, unlike Eliphaz and friends. With certainty, God declared He was not happy with him or his friends. God told them to take seven bulls, make sacrifice, and ask Job to pray for them. God added as an incentive that if they did not, He would do what ought to have been done.

This must have been really difficult for them. They needed to admit Job was right and they were wrong about Job being an evil person experiencing God's judgment. Recognizing our error is a humbling experience that most of us avoid. Job prays for them, and God proceeds to bless Job. He doubles all that he had, and he lived another 140 years.

Now that we have covered the events that conclude the book, let us ask, "What have we learned about God?" As a story about God, what do the forty-two chapters of Job teach us regarding the God of the Bible? The exchanges between Job and his friends were consistently limited to a narrow range of issues. While they talked about many subjects, the focus was on four basic, essential truths: our relationship with God, our peace in life, our satisfaction with God, and our lack of frustration with ourselves.

The first truth is in Job 42:7. God is personal and relational. He spoke with Job and turned His attention to Job's friends. He called Eliphaz by name and spoke directly to him. We learn in the New Testament that we can be a part of God's family. John 1:12 tells us, "But as many as received Him, to them He gave the right to become the children of God." God's desire, God's heart, is relational. He wants to have fellowship with you and me, a consistent truth from the beginning to the end of the Bible. When God walked with Adam and Eve in the cool of the evening, it was relational. However, humanity fell, and sin separated God and mankind. Nevertheless, Enoch walked with God (Gen. 5:21–24). Abraham was a friend of God. David, born under the law, had a heart totally committed to God. He knew that his sin was against God and that restoration of relationship was not based on his actions or sacrifices but on his attitude of repentance (Ps. 51:16–17). Micah, one of the minor prophets, knew God was relational and was not moved by our performance. He lived during the divided kingdom. The temple, the priesthood, and all that pertained to it were still in place, but he declared,

> With what shall I come to the Lord and bow myself before the God on high? Shall I come to Him with burnt offerings, with yearling calves? Does the Lord take delight in thousands of rams, in ten thousand rivers of oil? Shall I present my firstborn for my rebellious acts, the fruit of my body for the sin of my soul? He has told you, O man, what is good; and what does the Lord require of you but to do justice, to love kindness, and to walk humbly with your God. (Mic. 6:6–8)

He made the point that all the requirements of the Law do not satisfy God. God's desire is fellowship and relationship. As noted in the last chapter, facing the cross, Jesus at the Last Supper told his disciples He did not call them servants but friends (John 15:15). Earlier, Jesus tried to comfort them. He told them that when they moved from time to eternity, He would have a place prepared for them so they could be together (John 14:1–3). God has always been personal and relational.

Our second major truth has been that God is gracious and merciful; He acts according to His own purposes. Job 42:8–9 illustrates this fact. God explained to Eliphaz what he needed to do to have a right relationship with Him. Contrary to his claim, there was an alternative to God's righteous judgment because of His grace and mercy. I trust you have experienced this truth. We enter into salvation by His grace; He moves in our lives to fashion, shape, and build the image of Christ by His grace.

Because God showed up at the end of the story and blessed Job, we have an example of God's awesome mercy in the life of one who trusted Him. Job did not deserve it; none of us deserve God's blessing, but God chose to bless Job. This is an amazing display of who God is. There is no way of explaining how he could become prosperous again; he lacked the health and the relationships to do so, as his friends had not been supportive. The reason Job was blessed was because God had chosen to do it. If he had not been blessed at the end, we would not know that God could or would do so. But God can bless us; He is the God of the impossible and the improbable; He intervenes and transforms lives. He is relational, gracious, and merciful.

We need clarity on a related issue. Some believe God blessed Job because he had endured and had done what was right. To such a notion, I say nonsense. Job's endurance did not have anything to do with what happened at the end of the book. He was blessed because God is merciful and gracious. Job made that point in every speech. God will do what God will do. For whatever reason, God blessed him. Job was a blessed man at the beginning of the book, prior to anything recorded. For whatever reason, He blessed him at the end of the book. It has nothing to do with the idea that Job has been good. He had not earned it, deserved it, or justified it. Our behavior does not motivate God. Blessings as a result of faithfulness would be inappropriate conclusions to the book of Job. Let us state it clearly: God did not bless Job because he had finally gotten his act together, making God think Job was then worthy. If that had been true, it would make us wonder why we were not being blessed and would contradict one of the major points of the book. We might ask, "What did we do? How did we sin? Why are we not worthy of God's blessing?" These are the wrong questions. God acts because God is God. We considered this with the blind man Jesus healed. It was the glory of God. When we challenge His right to be God, we put ourselves in a place of frustration, grief, and doubt. We question ourselves and God. We question His mercy and grace, but His grace and mercy are contrary to a performance orientation.

This leads us to the next truth, which has been addressed in previous speeches. God is not a God of performance orientation obligated to bless the good and punish the sinner. Job 42:10–15 states that God blessed Job. We cannot rationally claim or hold with intellectual honesty that Job's behavior deserved what God had provided. He is not impressed by what we do. God does not stand up and shout "Hallelujah!" when we read our Bible, pray, or perform any other positive act. He is not impressed by our good choices. By the same fact, He is not depressed by our poor choices and the dumb things we do. He is not thinking, *I cannot believe they did it again.* He is not wringing His hands in despair, wondering if we will ever get our act together. He is neither inspired to bless because we do right nor irritated to judge because we do wrong. He is not motivated by the nature, motivation, or character of our performance. God acts for His own glory.

Two passages of Scripture make this point. The first is Ephesians 2:8–9: "For by grace you have been saved through faith; and that not of yourselves, it is the gift of God; not as a result of works, so that no one may boast." Our entry into the presence of God is salvation, a gift of His grace. Grace is undeserved merit, favor, or provision on the part of God. If we earned it or deserved it, it is not by grace. It is grace because God provides it apart from our worthiness, apart from our actions, apart from our behaviors, apart from our earning or deserving it. God has graciously provided salvation. Some pat themselves on the back and are enamored with being children of God. They think God has seen fit to call them children because of whom they are or what they have done; it goes to their heads. The Galatians had this problem. This brings us to our second passage, Galatians 3:1–4.

> You foolish Galatians, who has bewitched you, before whose eyes Jesus Christ was publicly portrayed as crucified? This is the only thing I want to find out from you: did you receive the Spirit by the works of the Law, or by hearing with faith? Are you so foolish? Having begun by the Spirit, are you now being perfected by the flesh?

Paul makes a significant point. Our salvation came on the basis of what God did, and so does our perfection. Our spiritual transformation into the image of Christ and our consistent walk with God is also accomplished by faith and God's grace, not on our performance before or after we are saved. We do not become more righteous because we read the Bible, pray, attend church, give, witness, or whatever else is on our "spirituality" list. At one time, the list was don't dance, don't chew, and don't go with people who do. The list is irrelevant. God is not motivated by our performance. It was and always has been by grace. It was when we were sinners that Christ died for us (Rom. 5:8). God is a merciful, gracious God who does not act based on our good or poor behavior. He is not performance oriented, and never was. Grace removed Him from the realm of cause-and-effect spirituality.

Last of our four truths is that cause and effect does not control God. Job 42:16–17 tells us the end of Job's story and his earthly conclusion. Verse 17 says, "And Job died, an old man and full of days." There is no further reference to any aspect of his spiritual journey. That trip ends in eternity. Because of Job's life, God was not forced to act. He did not have to bless or punish him. Job's actions were not the basis of his spirituality or spiritual growth. We have seen this truth on several occasions. In contrast, this was one of the basic and frequent arguments of Job's friends. They observed that Job was suffering and concluded he had done something wrong. They argued repeatedly that God was a god of cause and effect: you do what is right and you will be blessed; you do what is wrong and you will suffer. Under that logic, because Job was suffering, he must have done something wrong. This cause-and-effect view of God was fundamental to their thinking. Previously, we considered that this was the foundation of religion and religious behavior. In the animistic religions around the world, you have to appease the tree spirits, the river spirits, the harvest spirits, or ancestors' spirits. If you do what is right, you will prosper. If you do what is wrong, you will suffer. It is the essence of what motivates religion. It was observed that too much of Christianity operates under the same errant views of God. Do right and God will bless you; do wrong and God will make you pay. That is contrary to the God Job knew and worshiped, the God of the Bible.

The life of Jesus illustrated this point. He was perfect God and perfect man. He was holy and correct in all He did. Nevertheless, He was beaten and crucified. We understand there is plenty you and I have done, but nothing He did to merit such treatment. He did good yet experienced evil. The martyrs of the early church illustrate the failure of cause-and-effect thinking. Because they were followers of Jesus, some of the Roman emperors decided they should be burned as torches in their gardens, fed to lions, or crushed to death in the drying skins of animals. The brutality they experienced was outside the limits of any cause and effect. Many over the last two millennia have experienced incredible cruelty, suffering, and death. Their good behavior did not produce blessing in their lives. While it may be a privilege to suffer for Christ, it does not seem to be a blessing. Their good behavior got them killed. This does not reject the truth, as expressed by Paul in Galatians, regarding sowing and reaping (Gal. 6:7). Natural consequences are a part of our world. If we do not have water, we will die. If we jump off buildings, we will crash to the ground. The natural flow of events does not establish that God's actions are controlled by cause and effect.

James understood this truth. James 5:11 says, "We count those blessed who endured. You have heard of the endurance of Job and have seen the outcome of the Lord's dealings, that the Lord is full of compassion and is merciful." If Job, as so many have contended, was a sinner God needed to reprove, this verse is nonsense. If Job was a whiner and complainer who was out of touch with God's desires and was causing problems, where is there any meaning to this comment regarding the endurance of Job? He was not enduring! He was enduring only if his relationship with God and his commitment to Him had been consistent. Because of his relationship with God, he had been waiting on God to move in grace and mercy. This is the only understanding that makes sense of James' statement. Job's heart was right with God; he knew who God was. Job rejected performance-based religion as well as cause-and-effect spirituality. Because Job knew God, he endured the experiences of life. In patience he waited for God to act according to His purposes, not his own desires.

We have come to the end of Job. We have read the arguments of Job's friends and the responses he gave. We considered God's intervention and concluded that Job was right with God and his friends were not. God is personal and relational. He is gracious and merciful; He acts according to His own purposes. God is not performance oriented. He is not controlled by cause-and effect-spirituality. We will find a growing peace in our lives as we apply these truths to the circumstances we face.

In 1 Corinthians 10:13, we learn that when we are struggling and in the grip of temptation, "No temptation has overtaken you but such as is common to man; and God is faithful, who will not allow you to be tempted beyond what you are able, but with the temptation will provide the way of escape also, so that you will be able to endure it." God made that provision for Job, and He will make that provision for you. As we walk with Him, let us remind ourselves that our fellowship is the desire of God's heart. Let us enjoy our walk with Him, daily and personally. Through all the experiences of life, He shares them with us. God is there and nothing can separate us from His love (Rom 8:37–39). You are His champion.

Epilogue

Job has been a book about the character of God. I suggested at the beginning you read this book with a heart thirsting to know Him better, and you have stuck with it all the way to the end. That leaves the question, do you know Him better? Hopefully, it has become obvious why God would have chosen Job to be His champion in this epic challenge with Satan. Job knew the God he worshiped, the God of the Bible. Amazingly, he had none of the advantages we do that inform us of the awesomeness of God. Here are six important lessons from Job:

- The conditions of your life do not say anything about your relationship with God. Job was wealthy and in good health, and then he was poor and in failing health, but his relationship with God was the same. When he was poor and in failing health, he was God's champion in the spiritual battle with Satan.

- Because God understood our commitment to sin, He knew He had to act. He needed to mediate the relationship. He needed to be able to lay His hand on both parties. Jesus needed to become flesh to share in our humanity to be our mediator.

- God wants to have a relationship with you. Jesus told the disciples it was a friendship. A relationship has more to do with time spent than action taken. We need to spend time with God to learn who He is and what He likes. Too many are busy doing what they think He wants rather than getting to know Him.

- Because our relationships are based on what He did, our actions do not motivate His behavior. He operates for His glory, not ours. We cannot cause Him to love us more or less. If we are trying to gain something from God by our actions, we do not understand the God of the Bible. The potter controls the pot; the pot does not control the potter.

- I heard a story recently about a guy who was complaining to God about the failed lives and lack of character in the people who were serving Him. God's response was, "That is the only kind I have to work with." We need to repent of our arrogance if we think God is impressed with who we are or what we can do. It is walking humbly with God. He uses the foolish things of the world (1 Cor. 1:27).

- Suffering may be a part of God's plan for your life as it was for Paul (Acts 9:16). Peter understood God makes that decision (1 Pet. 2:20, 3:14, 3:17, 4:19). The hatred of the world will bring suffering into our lives (John 15:18–19).

Appendix A

Suffering and a Good God

Some believe Job brought his troubles on himself. A frequent source of proof is his statement, "What I fear comes upon me" (Job 3:25). Some claim Job's fears gave Satan the ground necessary to attack him, that if he had not been fearful, Satan could not have attacked him. These individuals have a hard time believing a good God would allow Satan such freedom in Job's life if Job had not warranted it. God's goodness is one of His very basic characteristics; if God is not good, we are in trouble. The relationship between God and suffering is an important issue. If the book of Job is a book about God, there must be a satisfactory answer to that concern.

In developing an answer, there are two avenues to explore. First, we must look at the story, and then we must look at three other lives in the Bible. However, before we consider these, we must answer an important question regarding our view of the Bible. Do we understand the Bible based on our theology, or do we understand our theology based on the Bible? If the Bible teaches something we do not believe, we need to change what we believe. Biblical Christianity needs grounding in what the Bible says, not what we want it to say. If Christianity is going to be different from other world religions, it needs to be God's revelation to mankind rather than their opinion of God.

Starting with the story, we find the statement at issue in Job chapter 3. At that point, Job is sitting with his three friends after he had lost all. One of the significant story issues is that he speaks in the present, not the past, because he had already responded to his past losses. "Shall we indeed accept good from God and not accept adversity?" (Job 2:10). If we reject the idea that God can be the giver of "adversity," we have a problem with God's statement at the end of the book, "You

179

have not spoken of Me what is right as My servant Job has" (Job 42:7). If God can be the giver of adversity, we need to rethink our idea of a good God.

This raises a more important story issue, the truthfulness of God. Did God tell the truth when He said Job had spoken what was right? God also said Job was a "blameless and upright man" (Job 1:8). If Job was a fearful man, God's statement about him was inaccurate. There might be a thought or a suggestion that a blameless and upright man might be an adulterer or murder. One could be described as a person after God's own heart, as was David (1 Sam. 13:14), without being blameless and upright. The first statement declares that a person does what is right; the other says that they seek God. Those are not equivalent standards. However, this was not just God's opinion; Satan seemed to share it. If Satan had the right to attack Job as a fearful man, he could have done that without God's permission in the early scenes of the book, but that is at odds with Satan's statement in Job 1:10. God was protecting Job; He had "made a hedge about him and his house and all that he has." So we need a reason for God to give permission, especially if Satan already had the right. His complaint that he could not get to Job would at least imply that Satan did not believe he had the right to attack Job. We also need a reason why God would claim that a fearful individual is "blameless and upright." God's truthfulness and omniscience are on the line. Did God not know everything? Was He being fooled by Job? Those would seem to be bigger problems than the perceived challenge to His goodness.

Another story issue relates to his fearfulness as understood in the objection. He would have had to fear losing what he had. He had lost his family, wealth, and health. That claim does not match Job's statement in chapter 1, "The Lord gave and the Lord has taken away. Blessed be the name of the Lord" (Job 1:21). That is not the reasonable statement of a person in fear of losing what he had. It also returns to the issue of God's truthfulness regarding the accuracy of Job's statements about God. Job said, "The Lord has taken away." Both Job and God are lying if you hold that Job was a fearful man. Job lied by attributing his loss to God rather than Satan, and God lied because He said Job told the truth about Him. If we accept the Bible as the Word of God, we need to believe both are telling the truth and to incorporate that into our view of a good God.

There is one more story issue to be addressed, the time frame with which we started. Job was speaking in the present after he had lost everything. I suppose one could claim because Job was going to become a fearful man, Satan had the right to attack Job. However, God still needed to remove the preexisting "hedge" (Job 1:10).

I suppose one could claim that because Satan knew Job would become a fearful man, he took God's bet. However, that does not help with the "good God" problem. This story is a debate and proof about why Job served God. Satan said it was about the "stuff" of life, while God said it was about the relationship. If Job was fearful about losing his "stuff," Satan won the argument. The second has the problem of attributing omniscience to Satan. If Satan had proven that Job served God only because of God's protection and blessing, the God of the Bible is a fraud, a far more serious issue than our understanding of "good." God knew His relationship with Job could withstand Satan's attacks and the loss of all he had.

Enough of the story issues; let us move to three other lives. The first is Daniel. Given the Babylonian approach to destroying an enemy, Daniel's experience would have been brutal. Initially, he may have preferred to have died with the majority of his countrymen. Death all around, captured, castrated, and imprisoned in a hostile country is not a blessing from a human perspective. If we are going to blame bad things on those who experience them, what had Daniel done? Early in his experiences in Babylon, we learn Daniel knew God, had a relationship with Him, and followed His directions. Nevertheless, later in his life, he was tossed into a den of lions, certainly not a blessing. What had he done to deserve such treatment? He had obeyed God rather than man. The only thing

Daniel had to do was worship and follow God to experience the attack of Satan in his life. While some might claim Daniel's misfortune was not due to Satan, we have it clearly on display in Daniel chapter 9. The fact that the "roaring lion" (1 Pet. 5:8) was not on display in every scene does not mean he was not present. Darius wrote after Daniel was protected from the lions, "For He is the living God and enduring forever, and His kingdom is one which will not be destroyed, and His dominion will be forever" (Dan. 6:26). It would be reasonable to conclude that Daniel's commitment to God brought honor and glory to Him.

The second life we need to discuss is the blind person healed by Jesus. The disciples held the same opinion as those who found fault with Job; they wanted to know if his blindness was due to his sin or his parents' sin (John 9:2). The assumption is that God will not allow evil to happen to good people. Some believe, though they may not say it, that God cannot allow evil to happen to good people. There is also the assumption that good or bad is a result of actions, attitudes, or decisions. At its core, this denies grace. If God cannot allow evil to the good, He cannot allow good to the evil, and we know that is not true. God sends the sun and the rain (good) on the just and the unjust alike (Matt. 5:45). More important, what did Jesus say? He told them that neither had sinned (John 9:3). The more substantive facts are that the parents suffered with a blind child and that this individual suffered a life of blindness "so that the works of God might be displayed in him" (John 9:3). There was a real controversy after Jesus gave this person sight. I think it is safe to say that God was glorified. Certainly, he worshiped Jesus (John 9:38).

The last life worth considering is that of Jesus, a sinless man attacked by Satan and eventually crucified by his design. Satan directly attacked Jesus in Matthew 4 when he offers shortcuts to the cross. Satan was a frequent actor in the gospel of Mark. We see Satan enter into Judas for the betrayal of Jesus in Luke 22:3. What was the result of a sinless life being attacked and crucified? The same as the other lives we have discussed.

God got the glory. Satan always got to play the part of Joseph's brothers. What Satan intends for evil, God uses for good (Gen. 50:20), and Job was no exception.

Was it good for a sinless individual to die? Was it good for a child and his parents to deal with blindness? Was it good for Daniel to be a prisoner in Babylon and be fed to the lions? Was it good for Job to lose everything? No! I mean, Yes! It depends on your perspective. One moment in time confirms or destroys the idea that God is good all the time. Jesus cried out from the cross, "My God, My God, Why have You forsaken Me?" (Matt. 27:46). In that moment, God is a good God or He is not. God turned His back on Satan's triumphant act of killing the Son of God. Paul asserted He is good: "He who did not spare His own Son, but delivered Him over for us all, how will He not also with Him freely give us all things?" (Rom. 8:32).

In each of these lives, bad things happened for the glory of God. They did not do anything to deserve or justify Satan's attack. We have the same choice Job and his friends had. We can believe that life is about God and His glory or that life is about us and what we get. Job believed life was about God and spoke what was right of Him. Job's friends believed life was about humanity, our actions, our attitudes, our possessions, and our families, and they did not speak what was right about God. A good God operates for His glory.

Having addressed the issue in context, we should consider one more passage. 1 Peter 3:16–17 says,

> And keep a good conscience so that in the thing in which you are slandered, those who revile your good behavior in Christ will be put to shame. For it is better, if God should will it so, that you suffer for doing what is right rather than for doing what is wrong.

Peter is very clear that we can suffer when doing what is right. His instruction is that we should rather suffer doing with is right rather than do what is wrong. Regardless of our view of Job, the good God of the Bible, the Jesus Peter knew, can make a volitional decision for us to suffer without a negative reason according to Peter. Our actions and our suffering are not correlated.

APPENDIX B

Regarding God

To discern the understanding of Elihu, let us summarize the differing views of God held by Job and his friends. Here is a summary of their positions.

The God Job knew:

6:24: One to teach how he erred

6:10: One whose words he has not denied

7:17, 18: One who is concerned about men

7:21: One who takes away iniquity

9:2–3, 14: One who does not accept self-justification

9:7–10: One who created

9:32–33: One with whom I need a mediator

10:12, 12:9–10: One who has granted me life

13:15, 16: One in whom I hope, whose presence I can enter

14:14–17: One who will resurrection my body

19:25–27: One who is my redeemer I shall see

21:22: One who judges, who knows everything

23:11–14: One I have followed

23:15: One who deserves my fear and respect

27:3–4: One I will not condemn

29:2–4: One who is my friend

The God of Eliphaz and friends:

4:7: The innocent will not perish; the upright will not be destroyed.

4:8, 9: God will destroy the wicked.

4:17: Man cannot be righteous before God.

4:18: God does not trust His servants and condemns the angels.

5:17–27: There is a direct cause and effect of blessing and condemnation.

8:5–7: Same as above.

8:13: The godless will perish.

8:20: God does not reject integrity or support evildoers (cause and effect) [Habakkuk].

11:13–15: The good are blessed; the bad are punished.

11:20: The hope of the wicked is to breathe their last.

15:14–15: Man is not righteous; God does not trust His holy ones; heaven is not pure.

15:20–ff: The wicked writhe in pain all their days.

15:29: The wicked cannot become rich or prosper.

18:21 (context): The dwelling of the wicked is destroyed.

20:15, 23, 29: God takes riches away from the wicked.

22:2–4: The active, wise, and righteous are blessed and do not struggle.

22:23–28: God will bless your self-effort.

25:4: Man cannot be just before God.

25:5: Creation is not pure before God.

25:6: Man is worthless (that maggot, that worm).

After reading through the two perspectives, it was necessary to determine which view was held by Elihu. So I created an additional list.

35:3: Job is accused of a performance view of God.

35:8: Job is accused of being wicked.

35:12: God has not answered because Job is evil. God does not listen to evil men.

36:5: The wicked are judged; the afflicted are delivered.

36:8–9: Affliction is a result of transgression.

36:11: God will bless right actions in this life.

36:12–14: God will punish wrong actions in this life.

36:17: Job is accused of judging the wicked.

36:26: Man cannot know God.

37:19–20: God is not approachable.

37:23: God cannot be found.

37:24: God is only to be feared.

37:24: God has no regard for the wise.

When you read through the list that expresses Elihu's view of God, it is obvious that it aligns with that of Eliphaz and friends rather than Job. Elihu asserted that Job has a wrong view of God when God said Job spoke what was right of Him. Elihu contended that God was not knowable, and Job claimed to have a relationship with Him. Elihu claimed that Job's suffering was a result of his actions and that if he repented, he would be blessed just like Eliphaz et al. Elihu believed and advocated a performance-based religion. The right things we say about God do not compensate for the erroneous claims that move us away from who He is.

Appendix C
Tried by God

Job spoke what was right about God (Job 42:7). The statement that God tried him (Job 23:10) must be accurate. Do we have a scriptural contradiction? James 1:13 says, "Let no one say when he is tempted, 'I am being tempted by God,' for God cannot be tempted by evil, and He Himself does not tempt anyone." At face value, this appears to be a problem. Some will make an issue of the original words "tempted," "tried," and "tested." However, they seem to be interchangeable and often the choice of the translator (see second-last paragraph). We need a broader biblical context than two verses that appear to be in conflict. Hebrews 12:7 is a good place to start: "It is for discipline that you endure; God deals with you as with sons; for what son is there whom his father does not discipline?" While "discipline" is a different word, even a different concept, it addresses the idea of God's action. This passage tells us that God will act in our lives in our best interest. Discipline is not viewed by the one being disciplined as a positive experience. This verse tells us that God will do things in our lives we may not appreciate. We may react, we may complain, and we may even resist; we probably will not like it. God will impose difficulties, challenges, and struggles in our lives.

The story we may struggle with the most is Abraham and Isaac. Genesis 22:1 says, "Now it came about after these things, that God tested Abraham, and said to him, 'Abraham!' And he said, 'Here I am.'" Does God test? The Bible says yes. That leaves the issue of "tempted" for some. I hope no one will argue that Abraham was not tempted to say no. He was probably tempted not to go to Mount Moriah. Certainly, we are not going to claim this was no big deal to Abraham and of course he would kill his son. Any struggle, difficult circumstance, or

189

situation presents its own temptations. A claim that Abraham was tested but not tempted is intellectually dishonest with our humanity and the broader context of Scripture and is in pursuit of an ulterior agenda.

God was willing to "test" Israel, His chosen people. For forty years they wandered in the wilderness. Deuteronomy 8:2 says, "You shall remember all the way which the LORD your God has led you in the wilderness these forty years, that He might humble you, testing you, to know what was in your heart, whether you would keep His commandments or not." God learned they were a rebellious people and did not allow them to enter the land He promised them. A few verses later, after describing some of the difficulties they faced, we read, "In the wilderness He fed you manna which your fathers did not know, that He might humble you and that He might test you, to do good for you in the end" (Deut. 8:16). God took responsibility for the lack of water and food and the presence of scorpions and snakes. God said they were tested. It is obvious that they were tempted because they failed to enter the Promised Land (Ps. 95:10–11). Semantics makes for poor arguments.

In 2 Chronicles 32:31, God tells us He tested King Hezekiah. It reads, "God left him alone only to test him, that He might know all that was in his heart." Call it a test, call it a trial, or say he was tempted; God did it, and Hezekiah failed. Hezekiah showed the envoy from Babylon all he had. That was a problem; it had devastating consequences. God could have sent the prophet to warn him but did not. God is not obligated to act to protect us from ourselves or anything else.

Let me add another dimension to this discussion. 1 Corinthians 10:13 tells us, "No temptation has overtaken you but such as is common to man; and God is faithful, who will not allow you to be tempted beyond what you are able, but with the temptation will provide the way of escape also, so that you will be able to endure it." This verse does not assert that God keeps us from temptation; it claims that God allows it and promises that there is the opportunity to face it successfully. The temptations you face are typical. Humanity deals with them all the time. Regardless of economics, cultures, ethnicities, or times in history, temptation is humanity's norm. The sins in the Old and New Testaments are the sins of today. Job's trials were not unique, but he patterned the opportunity for success.

Jesus experienced trials and temptations permitted by God. Some might say, "Show me the verse." With or without a verse, nothing happened in Jesus' life that god had not allowed. One cannot claim Satan snuck up on Jesus and engaged in a surprise attack; God allowed it tacitly or volitionally. Nevertheless, let me show you the verse. Matthew wrote, "Then Jesus was led up by the Spirit into the wilderness to be tempted by the devil" (Matt. 4:1). God actively, willfully put Jesus in the place of temptation. Some will argue that God had not tempted Him, Satan had. That is true, but God caused and allowed the situation. The distinction seems more semantic than factual.

Hebrews 2:18 tells us Jesus was tempted just as we are, and Hebrews 4:15 repeats the assertion. These verses promise us that because He faced testing without sin, He can come to the aid of those being tried. We need help, and Jesus can provide it. There was a reason why Jesus faced temptation; there was a reason why Job did.

Let us return to James 1:13. Better still, let us add James 1:2–4: "Consider it all joy, my brethren, when you encounter various trials, knowing that the testing of your faith produces endurance. And let endurance have its perfect result, so that you may be perfect and complete, lacking in nothing." There are two reasons for the importance of this verse. First, it is in the context of verse 13. Second, the same Greek root word is used in both places. "Tempted," "tempt," "trials," and "testing" come from the same word. Does that effect how you read these verses? We are tempted, but God is not. We are not to blame God for our failures.

Job had a very clear understanding of this concept. He understood that he lived in a fallen world and that bad things happened. He was very clear that he did not like it and wanted God to explain it to him because he understood that God was responsible for all that happened. Nevertheless, he was not going to blame God for his circumstances or the specifics (Job 2:10). He blamed the forces of nature, thieving marauders, and disease; he blamed his friends for their lack of understanding; but He did not blame God. A fallen world is a tough place to live. God's agenda is for our good and His glory.

Appendix D

Verses on Our Conversation

Here are some of my collection of verses on the mouth, lips, and tongue in no particular order. I noted these while I read the Bible; they have to do with speech, conversation, or communication. Some were directly relevant, others were obscure, but collectively they illustrate that God has a wealth of material on how we communicate with one another.

Let no unwholesome word proceed from your mouth, but only such a word as is good for edification according to the need of the moment, so that it will give grace to those who hear. (Eph. 4:29)

But now you also, put them all aside: anger, wrath, malice, slander, and abusive speech from your mouth. (Col. 3:8)

That if you confess with your mouth Jesus as Lord, and believe in your heart that God raised Him from the dead, you will be saved; for with the heart a person believes, resulting in righteousness, and with the mouth he confesses, resulting in salvation. (Rom. 10:9–10)

But immorality or any impurity or greed must not even be named among you, as is proper among saints; and there must be no filthiness and silly talk, or coarse jesting, which are not fitting, but rather giving of thanks. (Eph. 5:3–4)

For the mouth speaks out of that which fills the heart. (Matt. 12:34)

But the things that proceed out of the mouth come from the heart, and those defile the man. For out of the heart come evil thoughts, murders, adulteries, fornications, thefts, false witness, slanders. (Matt. 15:18–20)

It is not what enters into the mouth that defiles the man, but what proceeds out of the mouth, this defiles the man. (Matt. 15:11)

She opens her mouth in wisdom, and the teaching of kindness is on her tongue. (Prov. 31:26)

Let another praise you, and not your own mouth; A stranger, and not your own lips. (Prov. 27:2)

A lying tongue hates those it crushes, and a flattering mouth works ruin. (Prov. 26:28)

He who guards his mouth and his tongue, guards his soul from troubles. (Prov. 21:23)

A rascally witness makes a mockery of justice, and the mouth of the wicked spreads iniquity. (Prov. 19:28)

A fool's mouth is his ruin, and his lips are the snare of his soul. The words of a whisperer are like dainty morsels, and they go down into the innermost parts of the body. (Prov. 18:7–8)

The words of a man's mouth are deep waters; the fountain of wisdom is a bubbling brook. (Prov. 18:4)

The heart of the righteous ponders how to answer, but the mouth of the wicked pours out evil things. (Prov. 15:28)

A gentle answer turns away wrath, but a harsh word stirs up anger. (Prov. 15:1)

The one who guards his mouth preserves his life; the one who opens wide his lips comes to ruin. (Prov. 13:3)

With his mouth the godless man destroys his neighbor, but through knowledge the righteous will be delivered. (Prov. 11:9)

The mouth of the righteous flows with wisdom, but the perverted tongue will be cut out. The lips of the righteous bring forth what is acceptable, but the mouth of the wicked what is perverted. (Prov. 10:31–32)

The mouth of the righteous is a fountain of life, but the mouth of the wicked conceals violence. (Prov. 10:11)

If you have been snared with the words of your mouth, have been caught with the words of your mouth, do this then, my son, and deliver yourself; since you have come into the hand of your neighbor, go, humble yourself, and importune your neighbor. (Prov. 6:2–3)

My mouth will speak the praise of the LORD. (Ps. 145:21)

Set a guard, O LORD, over my mouth; keep watch over the door of my lips. (Ps. 141:3)

My mouth shall tell of Your righteousness and of Your salvation all day long. (Ps. 71:15)

Let the words of my mouth and the meditation of my heart be acceptable in Your sight, O LORD, my rock and my Redeemer. (Ps. 19:14)

Like a madman who throws firebrands, arrows and death, so is the man who deceives his neighbor, and says, "Was I not joking?" (Prov. 26:18–19)

THIS PEOPLE HONORS ME WITH THEIR LIPS, BUT THEIR HEART IS FAR AWAY FROM ME. (Matt 15:8)

A fool's mouth is his ruin, and his lips are the snare of his soul. (Prov. 18:7)

An evildoer listens to wicked lips; a liar pays attention to a destructive tongue. (Prov. 17:4)

CPSIA information can be obtained at www.ICGtesting.com
Printed in the USA
LVOW13102200613

339483LV00001B/13/P